# The Disappearance of Steven Koecher: An anthology of True Crime

Pete Dove

Published by Trellis Publishing, 2021.

THE DISAPPEARANCE OF STEVEN KOECHER: AN ANTHOLOGY OF TRUE CRIME

**First edition. July 8, 2021.**

Copyright © 2021 Pete Dove.

ISBN: 979-8224091256

Written by Pete Dove.

# The Disappearance of Steven Koecher

**Pete Dove**

**The Strangest Disappearance**

When a person goes missing, the tragic consequences spread far. Family, friends, even investigators, become affected by the loss. Guilt, hope, fear, panic and other emotions equally as painful inhabit every waking moment of those who are most closely impacted by the incident. For all that, there is no denying that when it is a child who disappears, or a young woman, or mother of small children, the attention given by the media is greater than it is for a person who does not pull at the nation's heartstrings. Especially, for example, a man who holds no family responsibilities.

That is why, in all probability, few readers will be familiar with the case of Steven Koecher. But while his loss might be less well known than many, it is no less tragic. Steven was thirty, single and effectively out of work. A college graduate down on his luck. Right at the bottom of the list of people who might garner pages in the media, or online. Certainly, the mysterious circumstances of his disappearance have earned his case a couple of TV outings. His disappearance has been covered on the cable TV show Investigation Discovery, and episode two of season four of the true crime documentary series Disappeared also features Steven. But compared with many missing people, his story is little told.

Therefore, everything that can be done to keep his tale alive must be tried. Perhaps, who knows, an account might spur a memory or jog an action; encourage somebody with a half forgotten, apparently innocuous piece of information to make contact with the authorities.

Steven was last seen in 2009. Christmas was closing in, and his car was loaded with wrapped presents. It was a little before midday, PST, on Sunday December 13th, when a home CCTV security set captured Steven leaving his car, which was parked at the end of a cul de sac in Henderson, Nevada. Whether by chance or intent, he had picked a spot to leave his car where it was likely to be secure. The Anthem region of Henderson he had chosen is one of the most affluent suburbs in the Las Vegas Valley. The planned community, just a fraction over ten years old at the point he pulled his car up for the final time, is home to comfortably off professionals and wealthy retirees. Average household income in the area runs to nearly $150000. It is a region where private schools proliferate, matching the number of public schools provided by the Clark County School District. Whether his choice of improvised parking lot bore any significance to what happened next, we can only speculate.

A resident's camera picked up Steven leaving his car, then returning a few moments later to collect something from the vehicle. We see him walking away, and another of the many private security cameras providing silent security captures his reflection in the window of another car. Finally, a third camera, pointed through a porch records another sighting of Steven. We do not see his face, but the light-coloured trousers and jacket, plus the baseball cap, of earlier videos confirms it is him.

The footage is in black and white, but it is clear, even as it peers around the upright of the porch roof. It is 11.54 am. He is carrying a package under his arm. It looks about the size of a standard A4 envelope, or perhaps slightly bigger. He is holding it between his upper arm and body. Whatever it might contain, there is no attempt to hide the package from the occasional vehicle passing by. Presumably, this is the item he went back to collect from his car. He is walking along the tree lined residential street but although he is a long way from home, he walks with the purpose of one who knows the area. He is not checking a map, nor is he looking around, peering at landmarks. A couple of cars pass, but he seems unbothered by them.

He is walking quickly, but not rushing; he is walking in a relaxed manner, but not dawdling. It appears, from this contextless footage, as though he knows where he is headed. He makes his way along Savannah Springs Avenue, heading east before moving north on Evening Lights Street. Each of these is a tidy, quiet residential road.

Could he be headed for a post box to send the package under his arm across the country? If so, why pick a district such as Anthem? And why not pull up outside the collection point? Could the package be an early Christmas present for somebody he knows? But, according to his family and friends, he is a complete stranger to that area, and it would be a weird place to arrange a meet up. Steven disappears from sight as he passes behind a tree. He appears again for a couple of seconds, before becoming lost behind another tree – it really is a leafy suburb he is in – and then is gone. The most unsuspicious looking video work in the history of disappearing persons. That distant footage is the last sighting of Steven Koecher. However, it may not be the last evidence of his presence.

Everything points to the fact that he was intending to return to his car after whatever task had necessitated his purposeful walk. Not only were the Christmas presents there wrapped and ready to deliver, but they had been recently purchased, just a few days earlier. Inside the car, a six-year-old Chevy Cavalier, were pillows and blankets, and his shaving kit. Although no further sightings of Steven have been found, his cell phone remained active for another couple of days. At 4.36pm of the day he disappeared, either a call or text from Steven's landlord was picked up, the message relayed from the Arroyo Grande/American Pacific tower. That is some miles to the north of where he had decided to leave his car. Two and a half hours after that, an unidentified contact is sent, or received, via the Whitney Ranch tower. Then, a minute later, it seems as though somebody (Steven?) made a call from the phone, which pinged off a portable booster tower, called a COW tower. These are used to boost signal in areas where either the network coverage is minimal or has been compromised for any reason.

The next day, Monday December 14th, at four minutes past six in the morning, it appears that Steven (presumably) either contacted his landlord with a call or text or received the same from them. This is a remarkably unsociable time to make or receive a call. Then an hour later, at seven in the morning, somebody checked Steven's voicemail on the phone.

Although it was not used again, investigators believe that the phone remained broadly in the same area for the remainder of the day at least, most probably located somewhere near the intersection of I-515 and Russell Road.

Whilst Steven parked his car among the luxurious homes of Las Vegas Valley's wealthy, the Anthem development is not all multi-bedroomed houses, double car garages and privately educated children. There are some areas of deprivation, apartment blocks built to provide social housing, but which have deteriorated often into semi slums. It seems as though, based on the location of the towers which marked the journey of his phone, Steven was headed to these parts of the area.

Of course, it is not absolutely certain that he and his phone were still united at this time, but if they were, might this explain the package tucked under his arm? Was he delivering it to an unidentified address? An anonymous contributor to a missing persons' forum claimed to know the downtrodden parts of Anthem, or other parts of Henderson, and had this to say about the streets where the phone ended up.

'The apartments. You have to understand. I lived in two complexes right where his phone pinged, I am not sure if the phone merely pinged or he was actively using it. It seems he was in the apartments, but there's a chance he merely passed by. These apartments are extremely ghetto and filled with prescription pills. You cannot imagine.'

Might this offer an explanation as to how and why Steven disappeared? Was he the victim of an attack? What was in the mysterious package he had returned to his car to collect? Why, and how, did his phone end up in the drug infested hinterland of a wealthy, purpose-built suburb?

Up until his disappearance, Steven's life had avoided controversy. He was born to middle class parents in Amarillo, Texas in 1979. He was one of four children of Rolf and Deanne Koecher. A keen scout as a boy, he achieved the status of an Eagle Scout. Steven was – is, it is hoped – a devout Mormon. He did missionary work in Brazil and studied at the University of Utah, achieving a degree in communications.

He worked mostly in journalism, writing firstly for a paper his father edited, and then on to the Salt Lake Tribune, creating copy in their digital advertising section. He enjoyed the work, but not the night shifts nor the Salt Lake City winters, so after a year he relocated to St George, where the climate is gentler. However, his timing was poor, moving just at the point that the sub-prime generated recession was at its worse. Jobs were hard to come by, and he was forced to take low paid work handing out leaflets for a window washing company. Not the sort of job, it has to be said, commiserate with a degree in communications.

Although his lack of well-paid work sees him struggle financially, nothing seems especially amiss at first. But in the week before he disappeared, it appears as though Steven's activities gradually became, at best, strange. Yet the week started plainly enough. On the Monday he attends his Church's Christmas dinner, and the next day he is seen by his boss, who gives him $100. His job is low paid – distributing flyers for a window cleaning company. It does not cover his outgoings. The $100 would be a handy subsidy.

On December 9$^{th}$ matters begin to turn a little more confusing. He speaks to his sister on the phone but does not mention that the following day he intends to undertake a huge journey. It is a strange omission for siblings who are close. He spends a couple of hours at his church in the evening, then late into the night he has an uncomfortable phone conversation with his father, which ends, it seems, badly. The problem for Steven is that he is desperately short of money. He had moved to St George seeking job opportunities, but none of any quality had arisen, just the leaflet distribution work he was undertaking. That really could not cover his living costs. A month before, his home share partner had suddenly moved out, leaving substantial arrears. The two were not friends, or associates, simply two men sharing a rented house.

Reading between the lines of some pretty flimsy evidence, it seems as though Steven's landlord was unsympathetic. Steven's savings were gone, and he was falling in arrears with his rent. The landlord was calling frequently. He then committed the very unusual step of contacting Steven's father to report the arrears. Was his father a guarantor? Presumably, so, or at least an emergency contact. Steven's father phoned late at night to discuss the arrears and later reported that his son was angry that he had been informed of his financial problems. But that is not unusual, in itself. Steven, it seemed, was quite a proud man – he had been given a check from his Grandmother the previous month which he had not cashed. Now, at thirty years of age, he did not want his parents becoming involved in his financial problems.

But it is on December 10th that matters become very strange. He undertakes an astonishing round trip from his rented home in St George, back to Salt Lake City and from there to Wendover, Utah, and across the state to Ruby Valley, near Reno. He must have left home in the very early hours, because by 6.45am he had reached Salt Lake City and stopped to buy gas. He does so again three hours and another one hundred and twenty miles later, in West Wendover. Next, he visits an ex-girlfriend's home in Ruby Valley. She is not home, but her parents provide him with lunch, and he tells them that he is on his way to Sacramento, to meet family. However, they persuade him not to go, because of problems with the weather over the mountains. He agrees, and two hours after arriving heads back home, via Salt Lake City once more. Was this trip a genuine wish to visit family in Sacramento? Perhaps, but if so, Steven failed to tell his family that he was making the long journey. Yet, he did speak to both his sister and his mom that day. He phoned his sister an hour on the road back towards Salt Lake City but makes no mention at all of his travel plans, or even that he is on the road. At just before 7.00pm he phones his mum. He seems upbeat, even though he has been driving for more than twelve hours, and the apparent purpose of his journey has failed.

She tells him that she is looking forward to seeing him for Christmas, and that she has put some money into his bank account to help him with his rent. Despite his money problems of the time, he does not use that money. He arrives home at 11.13pm that night.

Records do not show his travel on the 11th December. Maybe, he decided to stay at home on that day, exhausted after his round trip of more than a thousand miles, which, with stops, may have taken him twenty hours or more. On December 12th he makes the short journey to Mesquite, just over the border into Nevada, and back again. Then on December 13th, the day he goes missing, he makes the 138-mile trip to Henderson.

The white Chevy parked on the wide turning circle at the end of the cul de sac was, it seemed, going nowhere. The local homeowner's association attempt to locate the owner, and the only clue they can find is the collection of flyers which can be seen through the car window. By the fifteenth of December, they decide to take action and call the number printed on the leaflets. Steven's boss picks up the call and passes on Steven's number. They ring and leave a message. With no response, they phone Steven's mother, and leave a message with her about the abandoned vehicle. Deanne picks up the message and contacts the police, reporting Steven as missing.

We can only presume that the HOA managed to get Steven's mother's number from his boss. But, once again with this story, great gaps appear in the timeline.

The police demonstrate only the briefest interest in what has happened. He is a thirty-year-old man. There is no proof of any crime. Nor, really, any suggestion of one. This is not a priority case. For the authorities, at least...it is of the highest priority for Steven's family, and friends.

The month after Steven disappeared, a number of family members headed for a pancake house on Boulder Highway near Flamingo. Reports had come in via a customer that a person fitting Steven's description was making use of the breakfast house, and they set up shop in one wing, hoping that he might visit while they were there.

Various staff members recognised photos of the missing former journalist. They said the pictures looked familiar, and described a customer whom they assumed was homeless, living off of donations from members of the public. But hope began to fade soon. There were no sightings of the missing man, and although there was a collective sense from staff that he may have been a customer, when questioned individually, answers were vague, and inconsistent.

As for the police, what could they do? A thirty-year-old man abandons his car and goes for a walk. It is not illegal to do so, no crime has been committed. There has never been any suggestion of foul play. Although the thought inevitably enters the minds of family, friends, investigators and other interested parties, the police have no evidence of such.

'It is still an open investigation. We are investigating it as a missing persons case and following all leads. At this point in time, we have found absolutely no evidence of foul play in this matter,' said Keith Paul, a spokesman for Henderson police. Mr Paul tried to explain the difficulties facing investigators with this enquiry.

'This case would be treated entirely differently if we had any evidence of foul play or a child was involved or an endangered person. At this point in time, we have an adult male declared missing, but we have no evidence of foul play,' he said.

However, Steven is registered on the National Criminal Information Computer, the NCIC, as a missing person. Yet, if he is discovered at any time in the future and says that he does not wish his family to be informed, then such a request would be honoured. He would simply be removed from the database and his thin file would be closed.

The case of Steven Koecher might have only provided tangential interest to the print media, but it has captured the imagination of those who can be linked together under the title 'armchair detective'. That brings benefits and disadvantages. The downside is that, compared to the professional media, there is less accountability for these amateur sleuths. Simply, provided it is not libellous, they can say what they want. Most don't; most home investigators are well meaning, interested people who can and do help to find missing people and solve crime. But these sources of information are never quite as watertight as with professional investigators or reporters. The upside is, of course, that such people are not bound by what their editor might permit, or their superiors allow to be published.

According to some online forums, Steven had been trying to settle his debts with his landlord. Slowly, he was reducing the amount he owed and apparently, he had a scheme whereby he would be free of arrears early in the new year of 2010. However, these forums suggest, by December he had stopped answering calls from his (admittedly persistent) landlord and ceased making repayments.

Certainly, the massive road trip on which he took himself on December 10$^{th}$ is hard to explain. Some family members had reached the conclusion that he could have been suffering from depression. He is in debt, he has moved to a new area, he cannot find a job (or, at least, one commiserate with his qualifications and talents), he is alone – although whether that makes him lonely is harder to determine. He certainly seems to be very committed to his Mormon church. But depression must raise the possibility that, like many men who keep their emotions locked inside, suicide was a thought running through his mind. Yet, if he had parked the car and decided to kill himself, three very significant questions raise themselves. Firstly, why in Anthem? Secondly, why has his body not been found – it is much, much more likely that a suicide victim's body will be discovered compared to, say, the victim of a homicide. Finally, why was he carrying the manilla envelope or package? Something sufficiently important for him to return to his car to collect it?

The location where he left his car might also be significant. Although none of his friends or family believe that Steven had any connection whatsoever to Anthem, he had chosen the only spot in the suburb where he could leave the car on a kerbside, but one that was not in front of a home. Maybe it was chance, or he had been looking for somewhere where his car would not disturb residents, but whatever, it was a remote chance to discover that spot unless he was looking for it. His phone then travelled for around ten miles. Was Steven still attached to it? Was the phone in a vehicle, or was its owner walking around with it? Had Steven been the victim of a mugging gone wrong? Questions, at present (and therefore likely to remain so) without answers.

Naturally enough, some of the armchair detectives who have become fascinated by Steven's disappearance suggest that his travels were connected with illegal activities, or at least, illicit ones. Was he delivering drugs? Buying drugs? (If so, what with? He had no money.) Yet there is no evidence whatsoever that he was involved in anything in any way nefarious. Steven was a committed Mormon; he did not drink or take drugs. He had a traditionally conservative outlook on relationships. Although, because no crime has ever been confirmed to have happened, the police have never investigated his car, Steven's family did. They hired sniffer dogs to check it out, and also had his computer and phone checked for anything untoward. Nothing came up, from any source. Some have pointed to the fact that he had no internet connection at his home and used the web in the Washington County Library for his browsing. They lean towards the concern that such activity is essentially untraceable. But it is, at the same time, extremely public. The chances of using the internet in a public place for illegal or anti-social purposes are extremely remote.

No, it seems as though Steven was no more than a good man down on his luck, who disappeared. The suicide theory, such as it is, also took another knock backwards in 2015 when the Red Rock Search and Rescue group organised used a methodological strategy to seek out his body, focussing on higher ground where his body might have remained undetected. The reasoning behind their move was listed as they were 'operating on the belief that Koecher travelled from St George to the Las Vegas area to do harm to himself; a search for someone who committed suicide.' Despite the scientific basis of their actions, no evidence of any suicide was found.

One theory which has gained traction over time is based on the fact that Steven disappeared at around the same time as Susan Powell, a missing woman feared murdered who lived in Salt Lake City. Her husband arose as a person of interest in the disappearance, partly because the two had been experiencing marital difficulties. On the night she disappeared, the husband, Josh Powell, had taken their two young sons camping. She was reported missing when she failed to drop her sons off at day-care, and police broke into their home, discovering two fans blowing on a wet spot on the carpet.

Josh Powell's family put forward the theory that Susan had eloped with Steven and tried to frame Josh for her murder. However, police investigated the theory and decided that there were no grounds whatsoever to support the claim. Another theory on Steven's disappearance biting the dust.

The theory has remained floating around more because Josh later killed himself and his two sons in a murder suicide than for any accumulation of evidence. However, it is hard to see what links Steven could have to the Powell family. That he had any relationship with them at all is based purely on the speculation put forward by the Powell family and that the two lived (relatively) close to each other and disappeared at around the same time.

We are left with no firm conclusions whatsoever regarding what really happened to Steven. He kept a diary, but nothing in it suggested that he was suicidal, or that he was thinking of giving up his old life and starting a new one. Indeed, the only points of even the slightest note in the diary are that he believed he would soon clear his debts, and also that his bachelorhood would soon be over. Given all of the above, it is hard to avoid the fear that Steven was killed on or soon after he left his parked car in the comfortably suburb of Anthem on December 12$^{th}$, 2009.

Perhaps the manilla envelope was something he had been paid to deliver. Could that explain the $100 given to him by his boss? Had he stumbled across something criminal, and paid for this accidental discovery with his life? There are substantial bodies of water in the area, and considerable amounts of open land nearby. It would be relatively easy to dispose of a body if one had the wherewithal to do so, and a mixture of remoteness and the natural world would take care of the rest.

Or did he fall victim to a mugging that went wrong? Then again, maybe, somewhere, Steven is still alive, living a new life and fearing every investigation into his past. Maybe, but it seems very unlikely. Every piece of evidence available points to the fact that Steven Koecher was a good guy, with nothing to the contrary.

Sadly for all, we have to conclude that the truth regarding what happened to him will probably never be known. It is right, though, that we keep on trying to find that truth. For his family, and friends. And for Steven himself.

# THE VALENTINES DAY MURDER

## ANA BENSON

Richard and Stacy Schoeck had a perfect marriage, or at least it looked ideal for their friends and family. Even though they have been together for a long time, they seemed to have eyes only for each other. Richard was Stacy's fifth husband and everyone was certain that he was indeed the love of her life. The couple still went on dates and celebrated their love in every way possible. So when Valentine's Day in 2010 came around, the Schoecks were setting up a romantic little getaway and a card exchange in a picturesque Belton Bridge Park which is located in Lula, Georgia.

Lula is a quiet little tourist town so when their Police Department received a frantic phone call with Stacy on the other end of the line, they knew something serious had happened. The town was shocked to discover that a murder occurred right there in their calm little oasis. But soon enough, the sinister plot started to unravel and the law enforcement realized that things were not as they seemed.

So what made Stacy Schoeck turn on her loving husband and who helped her with the murderous plan?

## Early life

Stacy Morgan was born in 1971 in Florida. Her childhood wasn't perfect at all and her father died when she was really young. This left a permanent mark on Stacy even though her mother remarried soon and she did have a father figure in her life. She was also molested during this time frame by an individual who remained anonymous to everyone around her. Stacy grew up to be a lovely teenage girl who would fall in love easily. She met her first husband while she was still in high school and the couple got married shortly after. Unfortunately, he wasn't what Stacy was looking for and it took her two years to come to this conclusion. She filed for a divorce and the two separated.

When Stacy was twenty years old, she met her second husband. Soon after the wedding, Stacy found out that she was pregnant with her first child. The marriage lasted a little more than a year and she once again filed for a divorce when her son was just a toddler. Instead of being beaten down by two failed marriages, Stacy remained strong and made a decision to improve herself. After all, she was only twenty-two years old. She applied for college and got accepted. Stacy moved on to raise her son on her own and earn a degree in psychology and nursing at the same time.

She managed to find the employment as soon as she got out of college. Stacy was still very optimistic about her love life and wanted to find someone to spend the rest of her life with. She met her third husband in 1997 but unfortunately, the marriage was short-lived once again. It lasted for only six weeks. Stacy decided to date casually in the future and gave birth to her second son in 1998. She was still a single mother but this didn't seem to bother her at all.

Stacy did need to improve her financial status and she found a better job opportunity at a clinic which was located in Atlanta. The family moved over there and she was ready to start over. She got an excellent position at the hospital's administration with the possibility of even better promotion. She would assist the doctors on a daily basis with various tasks. Stacy was a successful and independent woman who was capable of taking care of her two small boys on her own.

But something was still missing and Stacy was longing for a partner who would be there for her. She was tired of casual encounters and needed some stability. So in 2001 she married for the fourth time and moved out to a small town near Atlanta. She got pregnant once again and gave birth to her third son. She lived in a large house with her fourth husband and it seemed that her life was absolutely perfect. Her boys were happy and they loved the suburban lifestyle. On the other hand, Stacy was still unhappy. Soon after the separation from her fourth husband in 2005, Stacy met Richard Schoeck, a graphic designer who was slightly older than her. He was a patient at the hospital where Stacy worked at the time. The two hit it off immediately.

Richard Schoeck was an adventurer who lived his life to the maximum. Stacy was immediately attracted to his positive attitude and passionate outlook. Richard accepted Stacy's sons like they were his own and would often organize family outings that included the entire family. She loved how different Richard was from all of her previous husbands and thought that she had finally found the one.

Unconcerned about Stacy's previous failed marriages, Richard still wanted to make their relationship permanent. The couple did get married in 2007 but the ceremony wasn't standard at all. Stacy and Richard eloped and told everyone about the wedding once they came back home. It was in Richard's nature to do something so spontaneous and Stacy adored him for that.

Richard became a stay at home dad after the wedding and he would form a close bond with Stacy's boys. He was very involved with their school and hobbies so he ended up adopting the youngest two. He really did accept this small family as his own and wanted the best for the boys. Everyone approved of Richard and Stacy's family hoped that she finally found the man of her life. Unfortunately, this marriage would end up tragically in just a couple of years.

## The murder of Richard Schoeck

Prior to Valentine's Day in February of 2010, Stacy invited Richard on a small romantic getaway to the town of Lulu, Georgia. They were supposed to meet in Belton Bridge Park which is a secluded area near the town itself and exchange gifts there. This wasn't unusual for the Schoecks because they would often go on different adventures that were supposed to spice up their love life. The Police dispatchers received a frantic phone call sometime after the nightfall. Stacy was screaming that her husband was shot and robbed. He wasn't showing any signs of life.

The police arrived at the scene of the crime and sure enough, Richard's body was lying next to his pickup truck. The blood was both inside and outside of the vehicle which meant that several shots were fired. At least one bullet hit him while he was still in the driver's seat or getting out of the car. He crawled out, perhaps to run away or defend himself. The shooter continued firing the gun until they were certain that Richard was dead.

The investigators immediately closed off the area and examined the tire tracks which were visible in the surrounding mud. They noticed that the third vehicle was definitely there and that it left the scene of the crime prior to the arrival of Stacy. The law enforcement marked them as the evidence. However, there were some red flags that indicated that this wasn't a standard robbery. For instance, Richard's valet was still in the car and his jewelry was on him. Nothing was taken from the scene.

Stacy wasn't a suspect at the time but the police escorted her to the station in order to interview her and get as many details as possible. Lulu is a quiet town where crime rarely happens so the law enforcement couldn't zero in on any possible reason why Richard was shot. One theory suggested that he might have interrupted another couple at Belton Bridge Park because it was a common meeting ground for lovebirds who wanted to spend some time together outside of their homes.

## The interviews and investigation

Once Stacy got to the station, she started talking. She was asked to explain what they were doing at the remote park and she admitted that they did have problems in their marriage. She thought this would be the perfect time to add some flare to their relationship. Since Richard was a stay at home dad and she had difficult work hours, the two simply couldn't get any alone time to spend with each other. She was becoming desperate and unhappy.

She quickly admitted to having an affair to the shock of everyone who was present in the interrogation room. Her lover was a fellow co-worker from the hospital who was significantly younger than Richard. His name was Juan and he was a complete opposite of Stacy's husband. She needed intimacy and she fell in love with someone else who could give her everything she craved for. Stacy even took her lover to Las Vegas just a couple of weeks prior to the murder of her husband.

The detectives were interested in the affair and started asking questions related to the possibility that Stacy wanted to get out of her marriage with Richard in order to be with her new man. Stacy told them that she did think about leaving Richard but that no particular plans were made. She knew how much her children loved him and getting a divorce would probably break their hearts. They focused on Stacy's lover but she quickly debunked their claims by saying that he is not violent at all and that she cannot imagine him being involved with anything involving guns or shooting.

But Stacy did say that Juan knew about the rendezvous in the park so the police decided to call him up for an interview the next morning. Juan seemed oblivious to the events that took place last night and he told the detectives that Stacy claimed her relationship with Richard was open. This meant that each of them had someone on the side. Juan didn't seem to be bothered by this arrangement at all so the investigators started doubting their possible theory. Plus, Juan had a solid alibi for the time of the murder because he was in another city.

They were left without any solid lead in this case so it was time to look a bit further and include as much aid as possible. The park is a fairly isolated place but there was a nearby cell phone tower that covered the entire area. The investigators knew that if a call was placed from that location on the night of the murder, they would have the number listed. And it turned out that this was a crucial move made by the investigators because it would lead them in the right direction.

The list of calls was short because that cell tower is not in an urban area. The detectives used the contact information which was stored in both Stacy's and Richard's phones and they tried to find the match. Stacy's phone had the number that was called sometime around the murder. The contact info itself stood out because it said Mr. Results. The investigators were slightly confused because they had no idea who this person was. But calling him up would probably shed some light on the events that occurred on Valentine's Day.

The police quickly identified the mystery man who was present at the scene of the crime that night. His name was Reginald Coleman and he worked as a private fitness instructor in Atlanta. Coleman was born in Philadelphia but his criminal past led him to move out from his hometown and try to start over in another state. He was incarcerated in the past but managed to clean up his act. Coleman was doing fine financially and owned a fairly popular gym. As far as the local police force knew, he was staying away from any type of crime.

Todd Woodten who would become Coleman's attorney during the trial said the following on his client: "Reginald was a true survivor. He was street-savvy and always had a hustle going on. He did a lot of things for youth, trying to keep them off the street and keep them safe."

Once the police managed to attain the call records from Reginald Coleman's cell phone, they found the number he had called from the Belton Bridge Park. The investigators thought they would see Stacy Schoeck's digits but they were surprised with their discovery. Coleman called another woman - Lynitra Ross. The detectives then realized that the whole plot was more complicated that they initially assumed and that there are more players involved with the murder of Richard Schoeck. So how did all of them fit together?

After speaking to Coleman's friends, the police found out that Lynitra Ross was his ex-girlfriend who would often resurface in his life. But there was another detail that connected Lynitra to the murder – she worked at the same hospital as Stacy Schoeck and two of them were really good friends. Stacy was Lynitra's boss and a landlord. Since there was a third set of tire marks on the scene of the murder, the detectives quickly determined that the model did not fit the tires on Reginald's car. This did sidetrack them a bit but they were still determined to find out what really happened.

The investigators were certain that they did, in fact, have their suspect and that was Stacy Schoeck. However, they still had to connect the dots so they dug even further into the phone records of those three. There was a message exchange on the night prior to the murder of Richard Schoeck between the three parties. However, the most interesting clue was Stacy's bank account which clearly stated that she sent a total of $10,000 to Lynitra's account which she passed along to Reginald.

## The arrests

Since the topic of the third vehicle was still the big unknown, the police started going through all cars which were somehow related to Stacy, Lynitra, and Reginald. And soon enough they were onto something. Stacy did have one car which she sold soon after the murder. It wasn't registered to her but she did use it often in order to drive her relatives or get them groceries. They were surprised to find out that Stacy put their vehicle on the market but she told them that they will get a newer model as a gift from her.

The police became very suspicious of this story so they tracked down the new owner and took a look at the tires as well as the insides of the car. And yes, the tire marks matched perfectly. Stacy Schoeck borrowed that car to Reginald Coleman on that fatal Valentine's Day. The evidence against Coleman was piling up and he was arrested on May 25th, 2010. But as soon as the interrogation started, he denied any involvement with Stacy Schoeck or the murder of her husband.

Lynitra Ross was arrested a couple of hours after Reginald but she also refused to provide the investigators with any useful information. It was time to pick up Stacy as well so the police arrived at the medical center she worked at and led her straight to the station. The investigators had plenty of circumstantial evidence to accuse her of the murder and they didn't have to wait for her accomplices to start talking about the crime. All three of them were in custody and it was time to face the justice for their actions.

## Psychological assessment

Stacy Schoeck was put through a psychological assessment prior to the trial itself in order to determine if she had any underlying problems which were unknown to her or her family. The murder was well planned so she clearly wasn't distraught at the time which meant that Stacy knew exactly what she was doing when she asked her friend Lynitra to help her get rid of her husband.

The psychologists took a closer look at her prior relationships and marriages which ended in divorce. The reason for her unhappiness might lay in the fact that she lost her biological father when she was young and she was unable to connect to anyone. Not to forget that Stacy was also molested when she was just a child.

It was obvious that Stacy Schoeck was manipulative and knew how to get exactly what she wanted in every situation. Her intelligence was obviously high because she did put herself through school and successfully earned her degrees. However, her actions towards Richard Schoeck show that Stacy was also a sociopath because she hired a man to murder her husband and continued to live her life as nothing happened.

She mourned her husband publicly and got very emotional in front of her friends and family every time they saw her. The fact that she selected Valentine's Day as the date of the execution speaks volumes about her cold-heartedness towards Richard Schoeck.

## The trials of Ross and Coleman

The first of three to stand a trial was Lynitra Ross. She entered the courtroom in May 2012 and was facing charges for a murder. After all, she was a co-conspirator who helped Stacy Schoeck find the hitman who would eventually pull the trigger and take Richard's life. Stacy was also present in the courtroom but she wasn't the accused in this situation. As a matter of fact, she testified on the side of the prosecution.

Stacy Schoeck was cooperating with the law enforcement and made a deal regarding her sentencing. She did everything to avoid the death penalty and was ready to talk about the murder of her husband. It was clear that her deeds were out in the open and she said the following as she took the stand: "I'm going to testify truthfully for Richard. It's all I can give his mom and his family and the children — all I can give them is the truth."

The jury then heard the story about the murder plot. Stacy Schoeck had the idea to take her husband's life in December 2009 after she noticed that her boys were acting strangely. They were getting into troubles and she started to suspect that they might be victims of molestation. She remembered how she behaved during the time she was assaulted as a child and found the connection. Of course, her first suspect was Richard because he was always with the boys.

Stacy also said: "I was just so fixated in my mind that Richard was doing something wrong that I said, 'I don't want the cops, I don't want a divorce, I want him dead.'" She then admitted to asking an unnamed man to help her kill her husband but he stopped returning her calls. Then she talked to her friend and co-worker Lynitra Ross and told her about her suspicions. Lynitra responded with the suggestion that they talk to her ex-boyfriend who would know what to do because he was "an experienced hitman".

After Lynitra Ross contacted Coleman, the two woman drove to his house and sat down with him in order to agree on some finer details regarding the hit. They talked and ate food from Zaxby's. Stacy suggested the park as the perfect place for executing her husband because he wouldn't suspect a thing. Reginald and Stacy agreed on the amount of money she would pay him for the murder, as well as on the vehicle he would take to the park. All three of them went to Belton Bridge Park so that Stacy could show him the exact place where her husband will be waiting.

Stacy noted in her testimony the following: "The only times I ever saw or spoke to Reginald Coleman was the day we had Zaxby's that afternoon and the following Saturday when we went up to Belton

Bridge. Everything else was done through Lynitra." She also added that she had given Lynitra the property she was renting to her as the payment for the help.

Lynitra's defense lawyers took the stand and told the jury that Stacy's testimony which involved the molestation claims was slightly off due to the fact that she admitted to having an affair in the first interview she gave after the murder. She didn't mention anything related to the possible sexual abuse of her children.

In August of 2012, Lynitra Ross was sentenced to life in prison. There would be no possibility of a parole either. Even though she didn't pull the trigger, she was the person who set up Stacy and Reginald to meet. Therefore, she was directly involved in the murder plot.

It was later determined that Richard Schoeck didn't have anything to do with child molestation but Stacy's plan was already completed and her husband was dead. The investigators took her claims seriously and talked to the middle boy who immediately said that he never accused Richard of anything. As a matter of fact, he never even talked to his mother about the alleged abuse. However, this didn't stop Stacy's attorneys from building their case around this.

Reginald Coleman's trial didn't last long because as soon as he appeared in front of the judge in November of 2012, he pleaded guilty to the murder of Richard Schoeck. He also faced charges for owning the firearm as a convicted felon. Stacy Schoeck was set to testify against him as well, which meant providing the courtroom with the full account of Reginald's actions.

Reginald Coleman agreed to kill Richard Schoeck after he heard the story of the alleged molestation directly from Stacy and Lynitra. Since he grew up in foster care, he often listened to the stories from his friends about their own abuse. Coleman thought that he could help the boys have a normal childhood by eliminating the threat from their life. He pleaded guilty in order to avoid the death penalty which was already on the table if he went on a trial. Coleman received the punishment of life in prison without the possibility of a parole and some additional years for the possession of the firearm.

## Stacy Schoeck's trial

Once Ross and Coleman received their sentences, it was time for Stacy to appear in court for her own trial. The proceedings began in December of 2012 at Hall County Courtroom. Since Stacy cooperated with the prosecution in the trials of Coleman and Ross, the death penalty was off the table. Judge Jason Deal listened to the witnesses who described Richard Schoeck as a loving father and an exceptional friend who would never harm anyone. Stacy's defense attorneys once again repeated the story of the alleged abuse and claimed that her actions were severe because she wanted to protect her children from the aggressor.

When Stacy took the stand, she admitted to the crime and asked the judge to give her mercy. The defense told the courtroom about Stacy's own abuse and that she was acting erratically. However, the fact that the murder was planned months before it happened painted a picture of someone who wanted to eliminate her husband. Stacy had plenty of time to make sure that Richard was really the abuser and contact the law enforcement but she failed to do so.

Stacy's lawyers asked Judge Deal to consider giving Stacy a possibility of a parole and to keep in mind her troubled past. They also pointed out that Stacy was behaving well in prison and that she deserves a second chance. However, she received the punishment of life in prison without a chance to get out after serving thirty years which was the primary goal of her defense team.

Attorney Lee Darragh who led the prosecution said: "Judge Jason Deal appropriately recognized that Stacey Schoeck was the engine that put this train in motion, until the death of her husband. Without her involvement, this would not have occurred." The courtroom was filled with emotions because a large number of Richard's friends showed up for the hearing. One of the saddest moments was when Stacy's mother read a note which was written by her youngest boy which said: "I miss her every hour of every day, just like Daddy Richard."

Initially, Stacy Schoeck and Lynitra Ross were placed in two separate prisons in order to avoid any possible conflicts between the two but they were soon moved to the same facility – Pulaski State Prison. Stacy's family was left to wonder what was really the reason for this heinous crime because the exact motive was never uncovered. They got the custody of Stacy's three sons.

# THE MURDER OF ASHLEY FALLIS

## SARAH THOMPSON-CARLOS

27

What reason would a perfectly happy and healthy 28-year-old mother of two have for taking her own life? That is the question that seems to perpetually surround the case of Ashley Fallis, who was found dead of a bullet wound in the early morning hours of New Year's day in 2012.

A beautiful young woman, Ashley was small and slight, with a bright smile and an attractive face. A photo of herself on her wedding days shows her kneeling it the grass with her children: her two daughters, Madelynn and Jolie, and her son, Blake. Her blond hair is elegantly pinned back off her face, and there's such joy on her face. It's hard to imagine that this young woman, so vibrantly fully of life, would take her own life and leave behind her three children, all under the age of 10 at the time of her death.

According to statistics gathered by the CDC, over half of American women who are killed have relations to intimate partner violence. After analyzing the murders of women in 18 different states, spanning across the years of 2003 to 2014, the CDC focused on exactly 10,018 different female deaths. Of all of those deaths, 55% of of them were related to intimate partner violence. Intimate partner violence can be described as family members, lovers, boyfriends, partners and spouses. That that definition in mind, even more chilling was the finding that in 93% of those cases, the perpetrator was a romantic partner, either current or former. It becomes even more unnerving to find out that 54% of those deaths were gun deaths.

It draws the question, with a statistical trend like this, is it possible that an otherwise happy woman, with her husband and children, would take her own life? Despite what her friends and family knew about her, was it possible that Ashley Fallis was hiding a secret depression so deep that she took a gun to herself to end it all?

Most people can't say that they married their high school sweetheart, but Ashley was one of the lucky few who could. Unfortunately, that relationship didn't last. They married soon after their high school graduation, and had two daughters: Madelynn and Jolie. Despite the children, the marriage crumbled and fell apart, and the two divorced. It was in 2007 that Ashley met Tom Fallis, who would surely change her life. Tom Fallis was a responsible man, and he seemed to have his life together.

It was only one month into their new, budding relationship that Ashley fell pregnant once again. That was how Blake was brought into the family. Their son was what brought Ashley and Tom together, despite the shortness of their new relationship. It was only two weeks after Blake was born that Ashley and Tom decided to make their family official. Tom adopted Madelynn and Jolie, and they couple married.

As beautiful a story as it seems, Ashley's family felt as if the whole thing was moving quite quickly. After all, Ashley and Tom had only known one another for a month before she fell pregnant. Perhaps their relationship had grown closer throughout her pregnancy, and then after the birth of their son. Still, it was mostly unknown to Jenna Fox, Ashley's mother, and Joel Raguindin, Ashley's adoptive father. Ashley and her mother were extremely close, much more like friends than mother and daughter. Raguindin explained how they had tried to talk Ashley out of it before the wedding.

Tom Fallis seemed like an alright guy, at first. After all, he was ready to start a family. He seemed to have his life together. But, slowly, Ashley's family began to notice that there was something wrong with him. Tom Fallis had a problem with needing to be right all the time. He was aggressive, and seemed to always be ready to argue. Jenna Fox noticed it, and she didn't like it. Ashley's family was worried by the way Tom was acting, but there seemed to be nothing to draw the couple away from one another.

After the wedding, Ashley and Tom decided to settle down together with their three children in the small town of Evans, Colorado, just an hour outside of Denver. Tom took a jobs as a corrections officers at the Weld County Sheriff's Office, stationed at a local prison. Meanwhile, Ashley began working as a respiratory therapist. Those who knew Tom Fallis thought that he took the job as a corrections officer to feed his ego. After all, he was an aggressive person, according to Jenna Fox. He was also insecure. "He wanted total control of her," Jenna Fox told 48 Hours.

Jenna Fox also felt that she was a threat to Tom. After all, she was one of the only people that he could not isolate Ashley away from. The bond before mother and daughter was, seemingly, stronger than the bond between new husband and wife. The pressure to keep a balance between her new family with Tom and her relationship with her parents was put on Ashley. That pressure only increased when Blake, only just a toddler, was diagnosed with a brain condition. The condition was chronic, and would start to require almost all of Ashley's attention. Ashley was a doting mother, and did all that she could to give her son the attention and help that he required.

The constant attention that her son required, paired with the stress of Tom's increasingly controlling behavior was starting to take it's toll. Ashley was quite anxious, and overwhelmed with the situation as a whole. Still, Fox and Raguindin had never once suspected that Ashley was particularly depressed, nor did they suspect that she was suicidal. It just didn't seem like their daughter.

Still, Ashley and Tom's marriage was starting to feel the weight of that pressure. The two were considering a divorce, but apparently their relationship was slowly getting better as the holidays approached. The couple were planning a New Year's Eve party. And beyond that, they had received happy news. As the holidays closed in, Ashley had thought that she'd become pregnant again. They suspected that their family was about to grow even more.

That happiness only lasted so long. After she had gotten that positive pregnancy test, Ashley had stopped taking any medication just in case. After all, false positives happened all the time, and she wanted to make sure that whether the pregnancy was legitimate before she continued on. However, the day of their New Year's Eve party came and Ashley began to bleed. Perhaps she had simply not been pregnant at all, or perhaps she was miscarrying. Whatever the cause of her bleeding, Ashley had been excited for the new baby. Learning that she was no longer pregnant caused her some significant sadness.

Despite learning that she wouldn't be a new mother once more, Ashley and Tom went forward with their New Year's Eve party all the same. After all, the invitations had been made, and the guests were on their way.

The part was a disaster. Jenna Fox describes the way that the tension between herself and her daughter's husband was becoming almost unbearable. Fox told 48 Hours that she "knew that Tom hated me". Despite the friction between mother-in-law and husband, the party was beginning to wind down without major incident - that is, until Tom Fallis went into a blinding rage because he had overheard Ashley's uncle offering her some marijuana. He began to swear, furious and loud. He told her that she didn't need to get high, even if she was still upset about the miscarriage. He told her, "It happened," and then told her that they were leaving, and to "Fuck everybody," and just let it go.

As Ashley's parents were leaving the party, they observed as Tom went into the bedroom, slamming the door behind him. Ashley walked them out, and they said their goodbyes at 12:04 am, after the New Year's ball had already dropped. Fox didn't observe anything out of the ordinary about her daughter. She didn't seem upset by Tom's behavior, after all. It wasn't out of place for Tom to act like this, and become enraged and swear. As Fox and Raguindin hugged their daughter and said their goodbyes on the front porch, they had no idea that this would be the last time that they saw their daughter alive.

Ashley isn't here any longer to tell us the rest of her story. What we know of that night is what Tom Fallis claims happened, and the autopsy reports, and the police records. As they guests filtered out of the house, they were among the last to see Ashley Fallis alive. When the last guest left and the door closed, no one but Ashley and Tom Fallis really know what happened that night that lead to the death of Ashley early in the hours of New Year's Day.

According to Tom Fallis, Ashley came into the bedroom in a defiant mood, and he said that she told him that if she wanted to get high, then she would get high. Tom told police that he told her to do whatever she wanted. Tom told the police that he had been in their closet, getting changed, when he heard the sound of her loading a gun across the room. Supposedly, it was the .9mm Taurus that Ashley kept under her mattress. As Tom walked out of the closet, he asked her what she was doing - and then, he heard the sound of a gunshot. Tom claims that he ran across the room to where Ashley was and held her head where the gunshot wound was, then grabbed the phone and dialed 911.

A recording of Tom Fallis' panicked 911 call plays Tom's voice, panicked and screaming: "My wife just shot herself in the head! Please help me! Please help me!" While the 911 operator tries to get his exact location and calm him down, Tom's voice comes through the call, tinny and screaming: "Ashley, no! Ashley, no!"

Finally, as the 911 operator tries to get more information, Tom can be heard shouting at his dying wife: "You are not leaving me! You are not leaving me! Stay right here!"

All in all, Ashley's family had only been gone for ten minutes. Ten minutes previous, Ashley had been on the porch, saying goodbye to all of her loved ones after celebrating the incoming of the new year. Her parents weren't even home, yet. They were still on the road when they saw the squad cars that were dispatched due to the call made by Tom.

At the hospital, Jenna Fox told 48 Hours that she knew, from the moment that she had seen her daughter lying in the hospital bed, that Tom Fallis had been involved. Perhaps it was a mother's intuition. Whatever the reason, Fox had no doubt that her daughter wouldn't have committed suicide. Even with the grief of her miscarriage hanging heavy over her that New Year's Eve, she was surrounded by her family and loved ones. Fox didn't believe for one second that suicide was an option for her daughter.

Ashley Fallis hadn't died immediately from that gunshot wound. She arrived at the hospital with severe trauma to the brain. But she wouldn't recover. The last time that her parents saw her alive and sentient was on the porch, ten minutes before she took a gunshot wound to the head.

But what happened? Tom's versions of events are clear. Ashley came into the bedroom, angry, and took a gun to her own head. Despite the fact that statistics put female suicides by firearm at only 31.2% (compared to male suicide by firearm at 56.4%), is it possible that Ashley had chosen such method? Women who commit suicide are often going to chose a less painful method, and one that would not leave behind such a mess. Pills and cutting of the wrists are much more popular methods when it comes to women who take their own life. But perhaps it was Ashley's grief that had driven her to take her own life with the gun she kept under her mattress.

Was it?

Despite the fact that Tom Fallis called in a suicide to 911, the police thought that it was important to question him about what happened. The police brought Tom Fallis into the station early on the morning of New Year's day, leaving his parents to watch his and Ashley's three small children. While Tom's frantic 911 call had seemed genuine, the police weren't all too sure. Neighbors had reported that they could hearing yelling and arguing coming from the couples house. Being questioned by Detective Rita Wolf, Tom was immediately put under scrutiny. The wound on Ashley's head was near the back. When told that her wound wasn't consistent with a suicide shot, Tom simply replied, "Bullshit! I didn't shoot my wife."

When investigators searched Tom's body, they found scratches on his chest, which he had said were from himself itching at his newly shaved chest. But that's not all investigators found. When they went into the Fallis' residence to take stock of the scene of the suicide, they discovered something strange. Tom's version of events had Ashley coming into the bedroom in an agitated state, then simply going across the room to retrieve her gun from under her mattress and shoot herself in the head. The state of the house, however, was inconsistent with that story.

Investigators found that pictures had been strewn from their place on the wall. It looked as if there had been a struggle. Not only that, but divorce papers had been found placed in a drawer. Tom Fallis had insisted that things had been going alright with him and Ashley, and that while they had been struggling before, things were moving in the right direction. The mere presence of divorce papers seemed to speak volumes, going against what Tom Fallis claimed was going on in his supposedly happy family.

At the hospital, Ashley Fallis had bruises on her legs. All of the evidence that investigators were digging up seemed to show that something else had gone down after all the guests had left the party - and that it wasn't suicide. Still, even after Tom Fallis was questioned for hours, he was released later that morning without charges being pressed against him.

Raguindin told 48 Hours that he and Fox were "shocked that they let him go." Even more shocking was what happened after that. Detective Wolf had told Tom Fallis that she didn't believe that Ashley could have inflicted that gunshot wound on herself. The position of the wound at the back of her head wasn't consistent with a suicide. Still, on January 5th, the coroner made an official ruling, and Ashley's death was listed as a suicide. Officially, the case was closed.

That seemed to be that. Ashley Fallis, wife, mother of three and devoted caretaker of her special needs son, was said to have taken her own life in the early morning hours of January 1st, ten minutes after waving goodbye to her family on the front porch after their New Year's Eve party.

The story for Tom Fallis, however, would go on. He packed up his children and moved them to Indiana, where he would attend graduate school. Despite the stress and strain of the relationship between Tom and Ashley's parents, they were determined to keep in contact with him for the sake of continuing a relationship with their grandchildren. After all, they were the only pieces of their daughter that they had left.

Life went on. For two years, Ashley's parents mourned their daughter's untimely death, and maintained a relationship with a man that they hated for the sake of their grandchildren. It seemed like no one else believed that Ashley wouldn't have taken her own life, and no one else believed that Tom Fallis was at fault. Until, one day, two years after Ashley's death, a man named Justin Joseph caught wind of the case. Joseph was a television news reporter with a source in law enforcement. Turns out, Ashley's parents weren't the only ones who were perturbed by the case.

Two years had passed, but Joseph took on investigating Ashley's story, anyway. Nothing seemed to sit right, and it was finally time to bring Ashley the justice that she deserved. Months were put into interviewing neighbors and friends who had already been cleared by the police, all of their statements taken and their concerns brushed off. In April of 2014, Joseph interviewed one of the Fallis' next door neighbors, Nick Glover, and found just what he needed to bust the case of Ashley's death wide open again.

Glover's versions of events differed from Tom Fallis'. According to Glover, he had heard Tom come out of the house, so he knelt down beneath the window sill to stay out of sight while he listened. Tom's parents were outside, and Glover could hear Tom saying, "Oh my god, I can't believe I did it." When his parents pressed him for more information, Glover heard Tom say: "I shot her." Of course, this wasn't the first time that Glover had told someone what had happened. In fact, the day that he was questioned by Evans Police, Glover told exactly the same thing to a Detective Michael Yates.

Glover's mother, Kathy Glover, had gotten a phone call that night from another neighbor by the name of Chelsey Arrigo. She told them to call the police, because she was sure that Tom Fallis had just shot his wife. Arrigo had heard Ashley yelling for Tom to get off of her, and the pop of the gun.

Everyone seemed to know what happened that night, and nothing was done. In fact, Detective Yates hadn't even written the report correctly. In his report of the incident that night, he quoted Arrigo as saying Ashley shot herself, not that Tom Fallis had shot her. Yates had also claimed that Glover had never told him about overhearing Tom admit to the murder of his wife. With contradicting statements, no one knew why a follow-up hadn't been given. Arrigo hadn't even been interviewed, despite knowing that Kathy had been in contact with her the night of Ashley's death. The case had been handled poorly from open to close, and no one seemed to know why.

Joseph found another person who had heard Tom Fallis admit the the murder of his wife: a sheriff's deputy who happened to be at the scene. It wasn't until two years later that he came forward to tell the investigators what he head heard. It's unclear as to why the case of Ashley Fallis wasn't treated as a homicide, or why no one seemed to take Glover seriously when he had told them what he heard, or why the sheriff's deputy said nothing to anyone until two years after the fact.

Was it a cover-up by the police? Or was it simply serious human error that caused the police not to go back and re-interview the people who had said they heard Tom Fallis admitting to murder? It seems hard to believe that the police would simply brush away Detective Wolf pointing out the position of the gunshot wound on Ashley's head, and two witnesses who had heard Tom Fallis saying clearly, "I shot her." One would want to hope that it was a serious error, and not the police deliberately looking the other way. There's no explanation for why Ashley Fallis' death was ruled a suicide, despite the evidence of a struggle in their house, and the witnesses that described Tom Fallis has raging and angry that night.

Whatever the reason that Ashley's case was closed, it was Justin Joseph that got it re-opened. His investigating opened up some serious questions about that night, and why the police had moved forward to rule her death a suicide. The case was reopened by a Evans, Colorado neighbor, Fort Collins, along with their much larger police force.

Tom Fallis had more information for the police, too. Two years after Ashley's death, Tom Fallis came forward during the new investigation with a suicide note that Ashley had supposedly written. There were several notes, one which read: "Dear Tom [...] I'm sorry for your pain. [...] I am a failure at everything." Of course, the timing of the suicide notes were suspicious. If Ashley had committed suicide, wouldn't the notes have shown up that first night?

Finally, it seemed like justice for Ashley Fallis was going to happen. In November of 2014, a grand jury made the decision to indict Tom Fallis for the murder of his wife. He was arrested in Indiana, and his children were put under the care of his parents. Tom Fallis had gotten away with putting his wife's supposed suicide in the past for almost three years. It wasn't until March of 2016 that Tom was finally put on trial.

The defense used Ashley's history of mental illness, anxiety, and the pain of her miscarriage to build a case against a dead woman. They claimed that it was Ashley who had shot herself in the middle of a crisis that early morning on New Year's Day. They pointed out that Ashley had been drinking at the party, and that there was even a history of suicide in her family: her uncle's mother and brother both died from suicide by gunshot. Was this just another suicide in a long line of tragedies? The defense seemed to think so.

Still, when Ashley's therapist took the stand, he made it clear that he did not consider Ashley a danger to herself or others. Still, Ashley was on medications from other doctors that she didn't tell her therapist. Defense used that against her, and in favor of Tom - saying it was entirely possible that Ashley Fallis could have written those suicide notes without telling her therapist.

When Ashley's parents were finally able to take the stand, they insisted that Ashley was fine throughout the night. Despite her miscarriage earlier in the day, Ashley was among family and friends. Her demeanor only changed when Tom became volatile. Jenna Fox described, once more, how Tom Fallis swore at them all and wished for them all to die before going into the bedroom and slamming the door.

Nick Glover also took the stand, repeating what he heard outside of his window that night. Tom Fallis' parents, however, denied that Tom had told them that he shot his wife. Kathy Glover also reiterated the phone call she got at one in the morning from Chelsey Arrigo. Unfortunately, when Arrigo took the stand, she couldn't remember making such a statement to Kathy Glover. All she remembered was hearing some arguing. Apparently, Arrigo was intoxicated because of her own New Year's celebration. Weld County Sheriff's Deputy, Chris Graves, was able to testify that he also heard with Nick Glover had heard that night, which was Tom Fallis admitting to shooting his wife. Still, he was questioned pretty hard after admitting that he should have come forward about it sooner than two years after the fact.

Forensic evidence didn't fair well in Ashley's favor, either. It was determined that the gunshot would very well could have been self inflicted. And yet, the prosecution called forward a forensic expert of their own, Jon Priest, who explained the exact opposite: no, Ashley's gunshot wound could not have been self inflicted.

There was so much testimony and evidence that the jury had to go through. The conflicting theories from the defense and the prosecution told two entirely different stories about what happened that night to Ashley Fallis. When the Jury retreated to deliberate the case and make their verdict, it didn't take them very long. In fact, the jury was only out for about three and a half hours. When they finally came back, Ashley's family could only wait with baited breath as the jury read out their decision.

Not guilty.

Tom Fallis was acquitted on the murder of his beloved wife, mother of his children. Ashley's family still holds their opinion that their daughter would never take her own life, and Justin Joseph maintains that the entire case of Ashley's death was handled poorly from start to finish. There was reasonable doubt that Ashley had killed herself that night, and there was no follow up done. Still, even after all the evidence was presented, the jury could not find Tom Fallis guilty. Whatever happened to Ashley Fallis that night will only ever be known by two people: Ashley and Tom.

# THE MURDER OF BROOKE WILBERGER

OLIVIA WATSON

Chapter 1

May 24, 2004 is a day many people in Corvallis, Oregon will never forget. It was the day a drunk man who was also high on crack set forth to destroy a life. Joel Courtney set out that morning in his 1997 green Dodge Caravan in search of a young, pretty co-ed to fulfill his dark fantasies. He cruised through the Oregon State University campus, searching, failing. But Courtney was persistent, and his wishes were soon fulfilled after he came across the Oak Park apartment complex a block down the road.

On the same morning, Brooke Wilberger woke up without any inclination that this might be her final day on Earth. She was newly home after finishing her first year of University, and was enjoying how sunny the spring had turned out to be. She headed over to the Oak Park apartment complex, which her sister managed, to help do some cleaning and basic repairs. Her sister needed help washing the lightposts out in the parking lot, so Wilberger grabbed some rags and a bucket of soapy water and got to work.

A few minutes into her work, Wilberger noticed a green van pull up. Inside, a man was waving an envelope at her, trying to get her attention. He looked like he needed help, so Wilberger approached. When the van pulled away seconds later, all that was left of Brooke was the soapy water and her now-broken flip flops.

It would be more than five years before Brooke Wilberger came home, but she would never come home alive. The story of her disappearance was a twisted tale full of hope, but it would only ever have a bittersweet ending.

Chapter 2

Brooke Wilberger was born in Fresno, California on February 20, 1985. She was the youngest of six. With three older sisters and two older brothers, she lived in a busy household, but it was a pleasant place to live. Her parents, Greg and Cammy Wilberger, were devout

Mormons, and raised their children to be the same. The family was incredibly close-knit.

Brooke Wilberger grew to be quite a beautiful, accomplished young woman. Besides boasting a strong set of mormon morals, she also excelled in school and had a lot of friends. The tall, thin blonde also received a lot of attention from the guys in her school, but she seldom dated.

The summer before Brooke began high school, the Wilberger family left California behind and moved North to Eugene, Oregon. Here, Brooke attended Elmira High School, and met her first serious boyfriend, Justin Blake. Blake also came from a mormon family, and was devoted to his religion, so the couple got along famously. They respected each other's minds, bodies, and faith.

The young couple graduated together in 2003, and while they were both dedicated to each other, they were on different paths towards the future. Wilberger wanted to go right to college so she could better equip herself with the knowledge she would need to turn around and better those in need around her. Blake was ready to jump into missionary work.

Wilberger was accepted into the Brigham Young University in Provo, Utah, and when she set off for her freshman year there, Blake set off for Venezuela to participate in a Mormon missionary campaign.

Although she was separated from her first love, Wilberger could not deny how happy she was at Brigham Young. The University was owned and operated by the Church of Jesus Christ of Latter Day Saints, and was the largest religious university in the country. She was immersed in her faith in new experiences and knowledge. She was actively participating in something much larger than herself, and she loved it.

Wilberger kept in constant contact with her family while away at University. She would often call and tell them about what she was learning, who she was meeting, and what she was doing. Her favorite topic of conversation, though, was always the inspiration her surroundings gave her to do better for the world. Although she was excited to see her family after the end of the year, she was in no rush to leave the busy, bustling campus for small-town Oregon.

After finishing her classes for the year, Brooke returned home to her family in late April of 2004. Her parents still lived in Eugene, but she wanted to maintain some of her freedom, so Brooke often stayed with her sister, Stephanie, who lived an hour outside of Eugene in an apartment complex she managed in Corvallis.

Her family were ecstatic to have her back home, close by, where they believed she would be safe.

Chapter 3

On May 24, 2004, Brooke had been home for about a month. She was staying with her sister in the Oak Park apartments, which were just down the road from Oregon State University, where summer classes were already in full swing.

That morning, a female student of Oregon State named Randy was walking through the Reser Stadium parking lot when she noticed a green van driving around her. When it pulled up next to her, the driver of the van got out and asked Randy for directions. The student had a bad feeling about the man, and when she looked in the back seat of the van she noticed a bunch of empty boxes and blankets. Before the man could get too close, Randy excused herself and hurried off to class.

Several minutes later, another student, Crystal, was approached by the same van in the same parking lot. Crystal did speak to the man, who again asked for directions, but the conversation was interrupted by an athletic's coach, who Randy had reported the earlier incident to. When confronted by the coach, the van's driver quickly jumped back into his vehicle and sped off of the campus.

While this was all happening, Brooke Wilberger was a block down the road from Reser Stadium at the Oak Park apartment complex. That morning she was planning on helping her sister Stephanie do some routine maintenance work on the complex. She decided to start with washing the lamp posts in the parking lot, so she grabbed a bucket, filled it with soapy water, and headed outside. Stephanie saw Brooke hard at work scrubbing the lamp posts at 10:00 a.m. It was the last time she ever saw her sister alive.

Shortly after 10:00 a.m., the same green van that had been causing havoc on the Oregon State campus pulled into the Oak Park apartment complex. The van pulled up to Brooke, blocking her view of the apartments. He began asking for directions, but when Brooke drew near, he pulled out a knife and forced the 19-year-old into the back seat of his van and sped away.

Five minutes down the road, the van pulled over and it's driver, Joel Courtney, got out and bound Wilberger's arms and legs with duct tape. He also covered her body with blankets he had stashed in the back seat. After this, he sped off towards a nearby area that was covered with heavy forestation.

Hours after Brooke was snatched from the apartment complex, her sister Stephanie realized that she hadn't seen or heard from her in a while. She decided to track her down to make sure she was okay, and began with the place she had last seen her—the complex's parking lot. When she got there she was surprised to see an almost empty parking lot, save for the cleaning supplies Brooke had been using and Brookes flip flop sandals, one of which was now broken.

Stephanie immediately ran inside and called police, who immediately launched a missing person's case despite their protocol stating they should wait 24-hours first. Brooke's broken flip flops at her last known location triggered enough of an alarm.

When detectives arrived at the Oak Park apartments, they quickly discovered that her truck, purse, phone, and wallet were all still at the apartments. If she had left the apartments by herself, she had done so without any identification, money, and shoes. It seemed unlikely that this would have been the case.

The search for Brooke began in the same way most crimes do—with the victim's significant other. In this case, Brooke's long-term boyfriend was quickly eliminated because he was over 4000 miles away doing missionary work in Venezuela. Brooke's family was also quickly ruled out.

During this process, the word of Brooke's disappearance quickly got out to the community, and a massive volunteer search was launched by the Wilberger's Mormon church. Within days of Brooke's disappearance, both Eugene and Corvallis were covered in missing posters detailing Brooke's physical appearance and last known location. Over 4000 acres of heavily-wooded area outside of Corvallis was searched for any signs of the missing girl over eleven days. None were found.

Police soon began to realize that the best chance they had of finding Wilberger would be to find the person who had taken her from the Oak Park apartments, so they quickly began to focus on the few early leads they had in the case.

The method in which Wilberger was abducted led police to believe that her abductor was a repeat offender. It's difficult to grab a grown woman off of the streets without anyone seeing or hearing anything. Police began looking through sex offender registries and crime logs to create a suspect pool, one that turned out to include over one thousand names, all of whom were interviewed.

One of the first people contacted by police was 45-year-old ex-con Lauren Hugo Krueger. He had been convicted in 1985 for attempted rape and had served time for the felony assault and kidnapping of a 23-year-old jogger. Krueger had also been questioned in relation to several reports of harassment and stalking. Most damningly, Krueger had also been spotted at a car dealership less than a block away from where Wilberger was abducted from. It was a promising start to the investigation.

Chapter 4

Many police officers in Corvallis believed they may have identified the man who abducted Brooke Wilberger on May 24, 2004, as being Lauren Krueger. He had committed several similar crimes in the past, making him a likely suspect. However, when he was interviewed, police discovered he had an airtight alibi for that afternoon, and he was eliminated in the case.

Shortly after Krueger was eliminated as a suspect, another man by the name of Sun Koo King was identified as a probably suspect. King was an Oregon State graduate who was unemployed and lived in the area. He had recently had a lot of trouble with the law for breaking and entering into Oregon State dorm rooms and stealing their occupants underwear.

Detectives searched King's home and found a startling collection of women's underwear, used tampons, and pubic hair. King also catalogued where he found each object of his collection, which allowed investigators to see that he had gotten most of the items from dorms at the University and from the laundry room at the Oak Park apartments, the same apartments Brooke Wilberger lived in with her sister.

Police were shocked by what they found at King's home, but what shocked them more was that there seemed to be no sign of Brooke Wilberger anywhere. Further, King passed a polygraph test and seemed to have an airtight alibi. Investigators were again forced to abandon the promising lead.

By October 2004, five months after Brooke's disappearance, police had a third strong suspect—Aeryn Evans. Evans had been arrested the month before for attacking a Oregon State student on campus. Evans' step sister called police after the incident suspecting that he may have been involved in Wilberger's disappearance too, but this was quickly discovered to be impossible by police.

Frustrated by having to eliminate three great suspects in a row, police decided they needed to take a different approach in the hunt for Wilberger's abductor. They decided to focus in on the one piece of evidence they had directly connected to the person who took Brooke—a green Dodge Caravan.

Police suspected that the green van was connected to Brooke's disappearance because of the two earlier reports from Randy and Crystal on the Oregon State campus, as well as from a tip call from a man who identified himself as Brian. Brian told police that he had seen a green van driving around the area Brooke was last seen. The driver was acting suspicious enough that the van had stood out to the man. The three incidents were too bizarre for police not to connect with Brooke's disappearance on the same day.

Both Randy and Crystal were interviewed by police, but neither were able to give a clear description of the van's driver. They had both been too spooked at the time. However, the coach that had intervened in Crystal's encounter with the van had gotten a good look at the van itself and was able to provide police with more details, including the fact that the van had had Minnesota license plates.

While police were now convinced that the van seen on the Oregon State University was the van used in Wilberger's abduction, they still had no idea where to find the van, and no idea who had been driving it. By November, 2004, six months after Brooke's abduction, investigators assigned to the case were still on square one. Little did they know though, that another crime was about to be committed in Albuquerque, New Mexico, and this crime would lead them right to Wilberger's killer.

Chapter 5

On November 29, 2004, a 22-year-old Russian exchange student, who goes by the pseudonym Natalie Kirov, left the daycare she worked at on the University of New Mexico campus for home. Minutes away from her doorstep, a car pulled up next to her and a man jumped out and told her to get into the car. Terrified, she complied.

The man held Kirov captive in his car at knifepoint as he drove off. When they got to a secluded area of a dead end road, the man pulled the car over and began to sexually assault the young woman, forcing her to remove her clothes in the process.

After sexually assaulting the Russian beauty, the man declared that he needed a drug fix, a "pick-me-up," and drove to a shady apartment complex to purchase some crack. He left Kirov in his car, bound up with her own shoelaces. While her captor was inside, Kirov managed to free her hands and unlock the car. She immediately ran into the street, despite being mostly naked, and flagged down a passing car.

Just as Kirov settles into the car she flagged down her captor emerged from the nearby apartment. After seeing how terrified Kirov became, her saviours quickly drove off in the opposite direction and brought her to the police station. She was finally safe.

Police immediately responded to Kirov's report by visiting the apartments her attacker stopped in to buy his drugs. They were able to find a lady willing to admit that a guy named Joel matching Kirov's description had stopped by earlier that night. Further, she knew where Joel lived.

Police immediately proceeded to the address given to them and immediately spotted the red car Kirov described parked in the lot outside. Police had just begun examining the vehicle when they were approached by a man who said he owned the car. Police asked him if his name was Joel, and he immediately responded yes. Police responded in turn by arresting him.

The Joel police now had in custody was Joel Courtney—a 38-year-old mechanic fisherman. Joel lived in Albuquerque with his wife and three children, but his marriage was incredibly unstable. Only a few weeks before this arrest, Courtney's wife had taken out a restraining order on him.

When police dug deeper into Courtney's past, they discovered that he had a long standing drug problem that they were able to trace back to his childhood in Beaverton, Oregon. Courtney had grown up an average, loving family, but his life began deteriorating after he started using drugs at the tender age of 11. By the age of 14, Courtney began repeatedly molesting his sister and cousins, and by the age of 19, he began experimenting with satanism, and was arrested several times for sexual assaults.

Now, many years later, he was back in custody for the sexual assault of Natalie Kirov, but it had been almost 20 years since he had been committed a crime, something Albuquerque detectives were skeptical of. They wondered if he had victimized any other women who crossed his path over the years, so they contacted authorities in Oregon, Courtney's home state, to ask if there were any unsolved crimes that matched Courtney's modis operandi. Almost immediately, Oregon police mentioned the disappearance of Brooke Wilberger six months ago, hoping to finally provide some answers to Wilberger's family and the surrounding communities.

Chapter 6

After having Joel Courtney brought to their attention, the Brooke Wilberger taskforce in Corvallis, Oregon decided to look further into Courtney's past to see if they could connect him to Wilberger's disappearance. They were quickly rewarded for this decision.

Investigators soon found out that Courtney and his wife had only recently moved to Albuquerque, New Mexico. Before that, the couple moved around Oregon frequently looking for cheap accommodations. At the time of Wilberger's disappearance, the couple were living with relatives in Portland, Oregon, an hour's drive away from Corvallis.

Further, investigators found that Courtney had been working for a janitorial company in Corvallis while he lived in Portland. He drove the company's 1997 green Dodge Caravan with Minnesota license plates to and from work each day.

Courtney's van was the exact van police had been trying to track down for the last several months. Armed with this knowledge, police managed to track down the vehicle, which was immediately brought to Portland to be searched for any forensic evidence that may have survived. Specifically, they were looking for any DNA evidence to compare to known samples of Brooke Wilberger and Joel Courtney himself.

While investigators waited for the DNA results to come back from the lab, they looked into Courtney's whereabouts the day Brooke Wilberger disappeared. They discovered that Joel Courtney had actually been expected in court to face a DUI charge that very day.

Police learned that on this day Courtney apparently made a call from Corvallis saying he would be late for his court time, but he never appeared. Police also learned that the next day, a disheveled Courtney had shown up at a family member's house 16-hours away from Corvallis. When asked why he was in such a state, Courtney came up with a story of how he ran into a gang of men in the woods who had captured a young woman and forced him to do terrible things he did not want to do. Amazingly, the family member chalked the unbelievable story to Courtney's chronic drug use, and never asked about it again.

On the one-year anniversary of Brooke Wilberger's disappearance, Corvallis investigators finally received the results of the forensic sweep of the green Dodge Caravan. It was worth the wait.

The evidence recovered from the van conclusively proved that not only had both Brooke Wilberger and Joel Courtney been in the green van, but Joel Courtney had been the person to place Wilberger there, and he likely knew where she was now. The final challenge investigators now had was getting Courtney to reveal this information so they could finally bring Brooke home.

Chapter 7

On August 2, 2005, Joel Courtney, who is preparing to go on trial for the kidnap and sexual assault of Natalie Kirov is served an arrest warrant for the kidnap and presumptive murder of Brooke Wilberger. Weeks later, the Kirov case is brought to trial, and faced with the indisputable evidence against him, Courtney pleaded guilty. He was given a sentence of 18 years in prison.

But Joel Courtney didn't have long to get settled in the New Mexico prison system. In April of 2008, he was extradited to Oregon in order to stand on trial for the charges laid against him in Brooke Wilberger's case.

When the trial began in Spring of 2009, the prosecutors in the case showed the court Joel Courtney's long standing history of sexual assaults against women, which dated back to his late teen years. They also presented a witness that had seen Courtney the night before Wilberger's abduction. This individual stated that they used to work together, and that they had spent the night of May 23, 2004, drinking and smoking crack together.

Although prosecutors had a large amount of evidence against Courtney, they were missing something very important, something desired not only by them but also by Wilberger's family and the entire community of Corvallis and Eugene—Brooke.

Up to this point, investigators had been unable to find any indication of Brooke's final resting place, and Courtney wasn't about to give this information up easily. The Wilberger family was all but begging the prosecutors and investigators working on Brooke's case to make a deal with Courtney so they could bring their daughter home and give her a peaceful burial.

The District Attorney eventually succumbed to the Wilbergers' wishes and presented a plea deal to Joel Courtney. The terms of the plea deal stated that Courtney needed to plead guilty to all charges against him and reveal the location of Brooke's remains. In exchange, Courtney would receive life in prison without parole.

Courtney rejected this initial offer, but quickly returned to the bargaining table. Courtney offered to plead guilty to the crime if he could be locked up in New Mexico near his family instead of in

Oregon. He also promised to reveal the location of Brooke Wilberger's remains. Courtney's counter-offer was accepted and signed.

To uphold his side of the plea deal, Joel Courtney drew a map to Brooke's burial site for investigators and walked them through the events of May 24, 2004. He told investigators the story of how he forced the young woman into his van and took her to some nearby woods to sexually assault her. After being raped, Wilberger became enraged, and tried to fight her way to freedom. Courtney responded by punching Wilberger until she fell unconscious before beating her to her certain death with a piece of wood he found nearby.

Based on this confession, and armed with Courtney's map, investigators drove 10 miles outside of Corvallis to a heavily wooded area known as the Coast Range. Their goal: to locate Brooke's remains.

After several days of searching, investigators were finally able to locate Brooke Wilberger's remains in a shallow grave next to a clearing of trees. Her grave was hidden beneath a mound of tree branches and leaves. For the Wilbergers, the news was bittersweet. They finally knew what happened to their daughter, and they finally could bring her home, but up until this point they had always maintained hope that when she came home she would still be alive.

Joel Courtney was formally sentenced to life in prison without parole two months later, and was brought back to a New Mexico prison where he prepared to spend the rest of his days. It was the end of a violent sexual predator's freedom, but most importantly, it was the end of the mystery that had plagued Oregon police and Brooke Wilberger's friends and family for years.

Brooke was finally home and at peace, and the world was a little safer now with Joel Courtney now behind bars. This is little solace to those who continue to miss Brooke Wilberger dearly, but having some answers is inarguably better than none. Those who knew Brooke in life remember her as the sweet, caring angel she was. She had a good soul in her heart and a good head on her shoulders and would have undoubtedly achieved great things in life.

Brooke's family still keep in contact with the investigators that dedicated their time to bringing Brooke home—they attend the officers' retirement parties and exchange the occasional email—a small token of the gratitude they will always hold.

# THE MURDER OF CAROL TAGGART

## OLIVIA WATSON

On Boxing Day of 2014, a young man living in Fife, Scotland walks into the local police station to inquire about his missing mother, Carol Taggart. The young man is her son, Ross. Carol Taggart has been missing for three days. Her family is desperately worried, apart from Ross, who is still going out clubbing and hitting the town using Carol's credit cards.

Then police find Carol's body, devastating her daughter Lorraine and partner Shaun.

Growing up, the Taggart family were incredibly close. The family comprised of four members, Carol, the mom, Shaun, the dad, and Ross and Lorraine, who were brother and sister.

Ross is four years older than Lorraine and had a different father, but that never mattered to them. The two were very close as children, and Ross always looked out for his sister. Both were loved and cared for by Shaun and Carol.

Lorraine, who was both Shaun and Carol's biological child, was very close with her father. She was a daddy's girl. Likewise, Ross was a momma's boy, and proud of it. Ross and Carol shared a very close relationship, but Shaun always considered Ross to be his son through and through, and to Ross, Shaun was always dad. The two shared many happy father-son memories. Shaun had taught Ross how to ride a bike when he was younger; he had been there to take the training wheels off. They were a typical family of four.

Carol and her son shared a special closeness. Although there was always enough love for Lorraine, there was no denying that Ross had always been the favorite when it came to Carol. There was always a little bit extra love for Ross.

In his mother's eyes, Ross could do no wrong. To her, he couldn't lie, he couldn't cheat. Her family described her as believing that the sun simply shone out of Ross's backside. He was the golden boy.

But in his teenage years, Ross went through some significant changes. As a child, he'd always been a loving, supportive brother and son. He was outgoing, loved to meet new people, and always seemed to be smiling. When he got older, he became very introverted.

As a young adult, Ross never said much. He wasn't a man of many words. When he was displeased, he wouldn't speak up. He would just give an unmistakable look, and his friends and family would instantly know.

For his family especially, this was frustrating. They couldn't get into his psyche, or figure out what he was thinking. They would ask him why he behaved certain ways, but they would never get clear answers from him. Most of the time, they wouldn't get answers at all. Ross would simply give them a blank stare and go to hide in his room, isolated from the family and the rest of the world.

Ross knew he didn't need to work hard to be loved by his family though. He knew he was the perfect child in his mother's eyes, he'd always known it, since the day he was born. The pair had had years together to bond before Shaun and Lorraine entered their lives. They had a mutual feeling that it had always been just the two of them.

Ross was well aware of this connection, and he used it to his advantage. He used his mother's affection against her often, emotionally manipulating her to get his way. To those around Ross and Carol, Ross's behavior showed him to be lazy, unfair, and rude. He was a user and a narcissist. But to Carol, he was none of these things. He needed her, he was her only son, and he relied on her for everything. Ross eloquently played on every emotion Carol had.

Ross was lazy in life and expected everything to land in his lap. He was brought up in a beautiful house, went on beautiful holidays, and had beautiful cars. He was used to getting everything he wanted, so he saw no point in trying to work for anything. That seemed to be his outlook on life—why try when you know it will be provided anyways.

Ross's laziness wasn't a product of his upbringing. Lorraine, Ross's sister, grew up with all the same luxuries as him, but as an adult, she worked hard to make her parents proud. She understood the privileges she had and used them to better her life and become independent. Ross was the opposite.

In the eyes of her father, Lorraine was a roaring success. She worked hard in school, achieved high grades, held down jobs, and went off to college to study dancing, which had been a lifelong passion for her. While this was happening, Ross was at home cruising through life, spending most of it alone in his room or with Carol.

Carol always saw the best in Ross. She saw Ross's laziness as a struggle. She worked hard to please him, to make him know that he was her priority. Ross knew this. He knew he could use those feelings to make his mom support him financially. More than that though, Ross understood that he could play up his role as the helpless son to draw Carol away from other people who saw him differently, especially their family.

Carol defended Ross to no end when others tried to make Carol see she was being taken advantage of, but that wasn't enough for Ross. He wanted to isolate her. He wanted to be her entire world so the money and affection would never stop.

Carol and Shaun had very different ideas of how to deal with Ross behavior as he aged. Shaun wanted to be hard on their son. He believed that Ross, who was now in his early 20's, was old enough to learn how to hold down a job and stand on his own two feet. He thought coddling Ross was holding him back from being an independent adult, but Carol wouldn't hear it. She believed that it would just take time for Ross to come out of his slump. He would grow into a responsible adult; he just wasn't ready yet.

Shaun and Carol began constantly arguing about what to do with Ross. He had begun driving a massive wedge in between his parents. For years the couple argued, unable to come to any resemblance of an agreement on how to deal with their overgrown child. While Shaun was still adamant that Ross needed to become more independent, Carol began to aggressively prioritize her son above all else, even going as far as telling Shaun that Ross came before everything, including Shaun.

After 19 years together, Shaun and Carol separated. It was becoming clear to both of them that they were no longer on the same page in life, and there was no end to their fighting in sight. Both Shaun and Lorraine blamed Ross entirely for the separation.

Shaun was heartbroken by the separation, but there didn't seem to be anything he could do. He couldn't sit back and watch the woman he loved get taken advantage of by her son, especially when he was expected to submit to Ross's wishes as well. Reluctantly, he decided to move out of the family's house.

Now, the Taggart household consisted of Carol, Ross, and Lorraine. While Lorraine was saddened by the departure of her father, Ross was elated. He loved being the man of the house. Lorraine was disturbed by the new dynamic that was developing at home and left as soon as she could. She later described the two years where it was just the three of them together as the longest two years of her life.

After her separation from Shaun, Carol began suffering from bouts of depression, so much so that she was unable to disguise her sadness from her children. In her vulnerable state, Carol was even less prepared to stand up against Ross, who began exploiting her even more.

It was around this time that Lorraine began to understand the kind of person her older brother had developed into. He wasn't a lazy boy with no ambition; he was a user. He was bleeding his mother dry. Lorraine tried to warn her mom that Ross was taking advantage of her, but par for the course, she wouldn't listen. Lorraine was terrified that Ross was going to turn against Carol one day and that Carol would be left with nothing.

Lorraine tried to get her mother help for her depression. The more depressed Carol got, the more dependent on Ross she became, and Lorraine could recognize that that was a recipe for disaster. She went to appointment after appointment with Carol and tried to get her enlisted in different facilities. But this didn't help, Carol's depression got progressively worse. She was lost.

Lorraine recalls feeling incredibly frustrated with her brother during this time. While she was doing everything she could to try and help her mom, he continued to prey on her weaknesses. And for whatever reason, Carol continued to rely on Ross more and more, ignoring Lorraine's pleas and attempts to get her help. Lorraine couldn't crack through the glass that separated herself from Ross and Carol's relationship. As hard as she tried, she was always on the outside looking in.

After years of this, Lorraine couldn't take it anymore. She relented to the fact that Ross was always going to come first in his mother's eyes, and that there was little she could do about this. All she could do was try to make her mother proud by succeeding in her own life, and it was time for Lorraine to focus on this. She couldn't keep fighting a losing battle, so she left home.

Finally, Ross had his mother all to himself. Although at this point in his life, Ross was in his mid-twenties, he had no serious relationships outside of his relationship with his mother. He had cycled through a series of girlfriends, but unsurprisingly, none of them stuck around for long.

Carol, in her depressed state, also had a hard time maintaining relationships outside of Ross. She had no interest in dating, as she still had a strong love for Shaun, and she had little motivation to make or maintain friendships.

Carol and Ross's relationship developed into a non-sexual partnership. The two began going on holidays alone together, and they began spending all their social time together, it was the kind of relationship you would expect to see between a husband and a wife—not a mother and a son.

The more time the pair spent together, the more fused their lives became. Carol was now fully dependant on her son emotionally, but

Ross was still only using his mother to make gains for his own life, and Carol was completely unable to see this for herself.

Although the family of four had been close when Lorraine and Ross were younger, there was now a clear divide. While Ross and Carol were perfectly happy in their closeness, both Lorraine and Shaun found it incredibly strange. And they were no longer alone. Many friends and family members of Carol began questioning Ross's motives. There were very few people outside of Carol that saw Ross as a good man. To most, he was a bad apple.

When Ross recognized that his mother had become fully dependent on him, he began to exert dominant control over her. He no longer felt the need to be sneaky in his manipulations; he was comfortable being outright aggressive with Carol. When she disagreed with Ross or said no to him, he would get angry and withdraw, knowing she would work hard to get back in his good books, giving him everything he had asked for initially and more.

Lorraine saw the shift in her brother's attitude towards their mom and grew increasingly concerned. He was becoming nasty. His tone when he argued with Carol was sharp, condescending, and cruel. It sent the message that he was going to get his way no matter what.

Even though Shaun had been driven out of the family home by Ross, he continued to see Carol. The pair began to grow closer again, and Shaun worked to pry Carol away from Ross just a little bit. For a while, it looked like it was working. Shaun and Carol had grown very close again, and Shaun asked to move back in, thinking they had finally found a way to mend their broken relationship. But things did not go as planned. Before Shaun could move back in, Carol told him that she'd have to ask Ross for permission.

This set Shaun off. Throughout their separation, Shaun had continued to help Carol financially support herself and their children, as her depression had been making it difficult for Carol to work consistently. Shaun helped pay the bills; Ross did not. And Shaun and

Carol were adults. He saw no reason why Ross had any say in the matter. Shaun never moved back into the family home.

On August 11, 2012, Lorraine married her husband on a beautiful sunny day. It was the happiest day of her life, and one of the last happy day the whole family would ever spend together. Shaun proudly walked Lorraine down the aisle, and Carol, elated to be the mother of such a beautiful bride, was too swept up in the magic of the moment to care about Ross's dislike of her re-budding relationship with Shaun. The family was able to celebrate together openly. After this day though, Ross began to isolate his mother from the rest of the family further, something they all thought was impossible. When Lorraine had her first child a year later, Carol wasn't allowed to visit and see her first grandchild for over six months.

In October of 2014, Carol took Ross on vacation to New York City for his thirtieth birthday. Most people at the age of thirty have moved out of their parents' home, have started a career, and possibly even a family. But Ross's life couldn't have been more of the opposite, and he was pleased as punch about that. After they returned from their trip, Carol continued to indulge her son, spending over £1,500 on Christmas presents to give to him before the day even arrived. Unbeknownst to her at the time, Carol would never see Christmas that year.

Out of the blue, on December 23, 2014, Ross Taggart called the Fife police to report Carol missing. He told the operator on the other end of the line that he had gotten into an argument with his mom and she had simply walked out of the house. Because she had been suffering from bouts of depression for years now, he was worried that she had taken the argument too much to heart and had gone and done something terrible.

Investigators charged with looking into Carol's disappearance had several concerns about the nature of this phone call. While Ross sounded confident on the phone, he didn't sound worried.

Additionally, he had made a point of getting information across that isn't common when people usually report family members as missing. He seemed to be trying to set up a specific scenario; it was suggestive and manipulative. Unfortunately for Ross, manipulating the police was not as easy as manipulating his mother. Investigators were wary of Ross from the moment he picked up the phone.

Lorraine had not spoken to Ross in a very long time when she got a missed call from him while out shopping with her husband. She was nervous about why he was calling, so her husband called him back on her behalf. That's when Ross told them the news—Carol was missing.

Initially, Lorraine wasn't too worried. She was hopeful that Carol had merely begun to see Ross for who he was and needed to take some space from him and therefore wasn't answering his calls. She figured she would call her mom later, and Carol would see that it was Lorraine and she would answer. By the end of the day, Lorraine had called her mother over ten times but had received no answer. That's when she began to feel an overwhelming sense of dread.

Lorraine thought of several possible scenarios of why Carol had run off and wasn't answering her calls, and they all seemed to revolve around Carol's relationship with Ross. The most likely, she thought, was that Ross had hit Carol, and Carol had gone into hiding to protect him. Despite how little she liked her brother, Lorraine still never expected the truth to be what it was.

In the days after he reported his mother missing, Ross was closely watched by the police. His movements and actions were caught on CCTV cameras and were being monitored. In the late hours of Christmas Eve, he was seen walking around the caravan park where his mother owned a holiday caravan. A few hours later he was seen withdrawing cash using his mother's card. Even later that same night, he was seen buying drinks at a nightclub, again on his mother's dime.

After Christmas Eve came and went without a word from Carol, Lorraine began to heavily doubt her brother's account of what had happened right before their mother went missing. On Christmas Day, she got a call from the police. They had found Carol's car with her purse, wallet, and phone inside. At that point, they knew something terrible had happened. They knew she was gone.

On December 26, three days after reporting his mother missing, Ross went into the local police station to check in on how the investigation was going. The visit was captured on camera and showed the true lack of emotion Ross was exhibiting during this time. This visit raised further red flags regarding Ross's involvement in Carol's disappearance. There was no recognition of sadness in Ross as he eagerly asked questions about what the police had found out so far. He wanted to know exactly what the police knew, which made them feel like he was trying to figure out something more specific—were they on to him.

Ross's actions after his mother disappeared were suspicious to everyone around him. While his sister Lorraine and father Shaun were at home crying their eyes out, calling people, and trying to wrap their brains around what was happening, Shaun was carrying out his life seemingly as normal. He continued to go out to clubs and use his mother's cards on a regular basis, even buying movie tickets to see *The Hunger Games* at the cinema. He sold Carol's expensive jewelry, justifying the act by saying he was entitled to her estate according to her will. He was not acting as if he'd just lost the person who meant everything to him just a week ago.

By January 1, 2015, Ross was the sole target of the investigation into Carol Taggart's disappearance. The rest of Carol's family had picked up on this, as he had quickly become a topic of interest when police questioned them. Initially, it was just about Ross's behavior in the days following Carol's disappearance, questions like why is he still going out clubbing? Does he have permission to use Carol's cards?

But as time passed, investigators got less subtle with their questions. Eventually, they got to the meat of their queries and asked

Lorraine and Shaun the same question separately: do you think Ross would do something to Carol? Their answer was the same—absolutely.

On January 11, 2015, the Taggart family received the news they had all been dreading: Carol's body had been found.

Carol's body was found stashed beneath a caravan in the same park as Carol's. It was the same place Ross had been seen on CCTV footage stalking around on Christmas Eve. Her body told a horrifying story to police, a story of brutal violence at the hands of someone with nothing but hate in their hearts. She had been battered to death and throttled. Her neck had been broken, and she was covered in bruises. The damage was so horrific that when Lorraine was brought in to identify the body, she was only shown her mother's wrist, which had a distinctive tattoo on it, although decomposition hadn't yet made her face unrecognizable.

To both police and the rest of the Taggart family, Ross was the prime suspect. Above all else, Lorraine was angered that even in death, Ross discarded their mother. She was left outside alone, where it was cold and wet. He didn't make a mistake. He did not feel guilty. He had left the only person in the world who loved him outside in the cold alone for over two weeks, and he didn't seem the least bit sorry.

Three days after police found Carol's body, Ross was formally arrested and charged with his mother's murder. Lorraine and Shaun felt relief for the first time in weeks when they heard the news. It was unfair to them that Ross was allowed to live freely after taking the life of their loved one. They hoped that at least they could now get some answers from Ross on how he was able to commit such a terrible act.

As well as being charged with murder, Ross was also charged with perverting the course of justice after lying to police and taking measures to prevent investigators from discovering what had happened to his mother.

During his trial, which took place in Edinburgh in November 2015, the severity of Ross's attack on his mother became clear to Shaun and Lorraine for the first time. He had beaten his mother with his fists so severely that he had partially broken her neck. He then strangled her so violently that her neck snapped the rest of the way. It wasn't a crime committed from a distance. It wasn't cold and calculated. It had been done with his own bare hands, face-to-face with the woman who raised him, while she screamed out in pain and fought for her life. It was a lengthy, sustained attack, after which he wrapped her body in a sheet, put her in the trunk of her own car, and drove her out to her caravan where she stayed for several days before he went back and buried her beneath a neighboring caravan.

The case against Ross was overwhelming. Everything pointed towards him. The prosecution had been able to assemble hours of suspicious activities captured by CCTV cameras along with 188 witnesses and experts. Including Ross, the defense only presented two.

Just when the family thought they had heard the worst though, the prosecution presented a surprise witness whose purpose was to demonstrate further the lack of remorse Ross had for what he had done.

The witness was a young woman, who neither Lorraine nor Shaun had ever seen before. They soon heard that she had been contacted by Ross through the online dating app Plenty of Fish the night that he had murdered Carol. He was using the app to look for casual sex just hours after dumping his mother's body, unbeknownst to the young woman. To prove that the young woman was telling the truth, prosecutors presented the GPS log from Carol's vehicle. Both the locations of Carol's caravan and the young woman's house appeared on the log in succession.

As well as condemning Ross beyond a reasonable doubt, this information also provided insight into Ross's mindset the night he killed his mother. He was not remorseful in the least. He had felt powerful, dominant, and wanted to continue the adrenaline high he got from committing murder. He wasn't a normal human being—he was a psychopathic narcissist.

Despite the overwhelming amount of evidence against him, Ross took the stand in his own defense and denied having anything to do with the disappearance or murder of his mother. He stuck to the story he told police over the phone when he first reported her missing—she had simply stormed off into the night after an argument. His family, watching from the court, recognized the blank look on his face he always wore when he lied.

The jury in the case took less than an hour to reach a unanimous verdict of guilty on all charges. Ross received a life sentence, which meant he would spend a minimum of 18 years in jail. To Lorraine and Shaun, this was barely justice. He was set to be released from prison at a younger age than Carol had been when she died.

Carol's memory lives on in the hearts of Shaun and Lorraine, but their hearts will be forever broken. Carol had so much love in her, and it was incredibly difficult to see her taken away from them by the person that she loved the most. Ross had been her golden boy, she had given him everything she had and more, and just as those around her feared, Ross took everything from Carol. He took her money, her love, and ultimately, her life.

# THE MURDER OF DOMINIQUE DUNNE

ERICA THOMAS

**Destined for stardom**

In November 1959, film producer Dominick Dunne and actress Ellen (Lenny) Dunne welcomed a new baby to their growing family. Dominique Dunne was the couple's youngest of three children, and their only daughter. Dunne and her older brothers grew up surrounded by the arts – in addition to the influence of their parents, who were active in the California film industry, the children were frequently surrounded by celebrities of the 50s and 60s – close family friends who were often guests at the family home.

Dunne and her siblings grew up in a large house in Beverly Hills, but moved around fairly frequently as Dunne attended schools across the country – in Los Angeles, Connecticut, and Colorado. However, Dunne's childhood wasn't entirely carefree – when she was just eleven years old, Dunne's parents divorced. A few years later, in 1975, her mother was diagnosed with multiple sclerosis.

Still, Dunne pursued her education. After her graduation in 1977, Dunne studied art and Italian in Florence, at the Michelangelo School and at the British Institute. When she returned to California, she worked briefly as a receptionist and translator for Los Angeles' Italian Trade Commission before venturing back to Ft. Collins to study acting at the Colorado State University.

Her studies in Colorado were short-lived, however, and Dunne left after only one year to start auditioning back in California. Just a few weeks later, she was offered her very first film role. Dunne's acting career took off quite quickly – in her first three years, Dunne appeared as a guest on many well-known television shows, including *Family*, *CHiPs*, and *Fame*. And after taking on roles in four made-for-TV movies, Dunne made her cinematic debut as Dana Freeling in the movie "Poltergeist."

"One day, she decided to become an actress and the next week she was on a back lot making a movie, and that from then on she never stopped," said Dunne's father Dominick in a piece he wrote for Vanity

Fair in March 1984. "She loved being an actress and was passionate about her career."

**"At ease in a sophisticated world."**

To her friends and family, Dunne was known as a friendly, kind person. Despite having grown up with wealth and fame, Dunne's father described her as "totally at ease in a sophisticated world without being sophisticated herself." Indeed, Dunne dressed in casual clothes, preferring jeans and t-shirts to the upscale fashions her peers sported – and drove a blue Volkswagen Bug convertible.

Dunne loved cooking, traveling, baseball, and languages – particularly Italian, which she continued to speak quite fluently. She also loved animals, and had a soft spot for unwanted strays. Dunne adopted a cat with a lobotomy, a large dog with stunted legs, a snake, and a rabbit, among many other cats and dogs.

Even before her role in "Poltergeist," Dunne was a firm believer in supernatural phenomena, and friends say she was strictly superstitious.

**Instant attraction**

Dunne met John Thomas Sweeney in 1981, when she was twenty-two and he was twenty-five. Sweeney worked as a chef at Los Angeles' trendy "Ma Maison" restaurant, and Dunne was immediately drawn to him. After their initial introduction at a party that autumn, the pair quickly fell into a romantic relationship – and moved in together only a few weeks later, into a rental house in West-Hollywood.

However, their passion soon resulted in the first of many quarrels between the couple. Dunne was, by that point, well-known in Hollywood – a popular girl with many friends. Sweeney, on the other hand, had grown up poor in Pennsylvania, the product of a troubled family life. Despite Dunne's attempts to include him in her world, Sweeney felt like an outsider and was ashamed of his uncultured family history.

While Dunne had grown up with a loving family that respected and addressed emotional issues, Sweeney was raised in a coal town with an alcoholic father who, his mother claimed, often dealt with his frustrations by beating her – often in front of their children. By the time he was fourteen years old, his parents had divorced, and his father had developed epilepsy.

"Bitterly ashamed of his family and filled with a sense of worthlessness because he was a member of it, (Sweeney) longed to escape into a larger and more exciting life," read an article published in *People* magazine in 1983.

Sweeney's desire for a better life led him to pursue a culinary arts diploma from a local community college. At the age of twenty, he crossed the country to California, where he landed a job working at a restaurant called "Picolo's." Only one year later, he started as a chef's apprentice at "Ma Maison."

He was a talented, ambitious chef – and was willing to put in the work to achieve his career goals. After two years of double shifts, Sweeney was given a leave of absence to spend a year working on the French Riviera before returning to "Ma Maison" – where he worked as chef Wolfgang Puck's chief assistant.

His position at the glamorous restaurant gave him an opportunity to get a first-hand look at the elegant world he so desperately wanted to be a part of. And, after meeting Dunne, he finally felt like he would be able to access it. However, along with his excitement at being with a talented Hollywood actress, there was fear and insecurity – and the lasting sense of worthlessness he felt as a result of his troubled family life.

His jealousy started to take hold of the relationship. His interactions with Dunne grew more patronizing and dominating, and he began showing up on sets where Dunne was working to intimidate her male colleagues. Eventually, even that wasn't enough – Sweeney started to come to Dunne's rehearsals and even her acting classes.

It seemed Dunne couldn't do anything on her own without having to first discuss it with her boyfriend, which usually resulted in an argument that Dunne would never win. The more Dunne resisted Sweeney's possessiveness and jealousy, the more frightened he would be that she would ultimately reject him. Often, this fear would become anger.

**"Alex said he was scary."**

Dunne had introduced Sweeney to her family during the summer of 1982, flying the two of them out to New York where most of her family lived. According Dominick's article in Vanity Fair, Dunne's brother Alex was the only one who had "voiced his dislike" of her new boyfriend.

"Although I could see that Sweeney was excessively devoted to her, there was something off-putting about him," Dominick said.

The first night, Alex told his father about an incident that had happened after Dominick had left the restaurant. Dunne had been recognized by a man in the bar, who called out her iconic line from the film "Poltergeist." According to Alex, "there was no flirtation," just an excited, if slightly tipsy, fan.

"When Sweeney returned to the table and saw the man talking to (Dunne), he became enraged. He picked up the man and shook him," stated Dominick. "Alex said that Sweeney's reaction was out of all proportion to the incident going on. Alex said he was scary."

The next day, Dominick was to meet Dunne and Sweeney for lunch. Although he said he arrived at the restaurant late, the couple still wasn't there – and Dominick was already on his second bottle of Perrier by the time his daughter showed up with her boyfriend.

"I was immediately aware that she had been crying, and that there was tension between them," Dominick said. "The lunch was not a success. I found Sweeney ill at ease, nervous, difficult to talk to. It occurred to me that (Dunne) might have difficulty extricating herself from such a person, but I did not pursue the thought."

**Getting physical**

As the couple began fighting more and more, Sweeney's reactions frequently turned violent. On August 27, 1982, Sweeney reportedly tore out handfuls of Dunne's hair after grabbing it and using it to knock her head repeatedly against the floor. Dunne managed to get away from Sweeney and fled to her mother Lenny's house, with Sweeney following close behind. While Dunne's mother refused him entry and even threatened to call the police, it was only a few days before Dunne forgave her boyfriend and returned to their home.

Despite Dunne's forgiveness, Sweeney attacked her again not even a month later. On September 26, during another argument, Sweeney grabbed Dunne by the neck and pushed her to the floor before he started to choke her. Luckily, a friend heard the loud gagging noises coming from the next room – "it was the worst sound I had ever heard" – and came in to break up the fight.

"He tried to kill me!" Dunne cried out. Sweeney denied her accusation, insisting that Dunne come back to bed. Instead, she went into the bathroom, where she escaped out a window to spend the night with a friend.

The next day, Dunne showed up at the set of *Hill Street Blues*, where she was to guest star as an abuse victim for an episode of the show. According to accounts from cast and crew on the set, the bruises on Dunne's face and neck were "realistic" enough that she hardly needed any make-up for her role.

Dunne spent the following days in hiding, trying to avoid the abusive, angry boyfriend who was searching for her. Eventually, she contacted him to end the relationship – and to demand he leave the home they rented together so she could live there alone. Still, knowing how unpredictably angry and violent Sweeney could be, Dunne changed the locks of the house before moving back in without him.

### The final battle

That autumn, Dunne had taken on a new role – playing Robin Maxwell for the three-episode science fiction miniseries *V*. She'd completed filming the scenes for the first episode and was nearly finished with the second episode on October 30, when she invited her co-star David Packer to rehearse scenes together at her home.

The pair were hard at work when Sweeney called Dunne at around 8:30 p.m. – and then showed up at the house only ten minutes later. Dunne answered the door with the chain fastened, but Sweeney demanded she come out and speak with him. Packer asked if he should leave, sensing Dunne's discomfort with the situation, but she said she wanted him to stay while she stepped outside to deal with her ex-boyfriend.

Out on the driveway, an argument broke out. Sweeney was pleading with Dunne to forgive him and take him back, but Dunne refused. She'd reached her limit and was no longer willing to tolerate Sweeney's anger and violence. Like he'd done before, Sweeney suddenly reached out and grabbed her firmly by the neck, dragging her up along the driveway into the next-door neighbour's back yard.

Dunne was no match for Sweeney – the petite actress was a mere 5'1" and 112 pounds. Sweeney, 6'1" and close to 200 pounds, held her down and began to strangle her. She was unable to fight him off, and eventually fell unconscious.

Meanwhile, Packer watched the confrontation with growing fear – he could see Sweeney's obvious rage and jealousy. When he heard screams followed by a thud, he called the police, only to be informed that the location was outside of the department's jurisdiction. After hanging up with the officer, Packer called a friend and left a message on his answering machine explaining that if he was found dead, John Sweeney should be held responsible.

Eventually, Packer went outside to check on Dunne, and found her lying on the driveway with Sweeney crouched next to her. Sweeney asked Dunne to call the police, and this time, they said they would send an officer. When the police arrived and found Dunne still unconscious, they called an ambulance, which arrived only five minutes later.

## Brain-dead

On the way to the nearby Cedars Sinai Hospital, Dunne's heart came to a full stop, but doctors were able to restart it once the ambulance arrived. However, examinations showed that Dunne had sustained extensive damage from the anoxaemia during her strangulation – and that although her heart had been restarted, there was no way for doctors to reverse the death of her brain.

"There were tubes in her everywhere, and the life-support system caused her to breathe in and out with a grotesque jerking movement that seemed a parody of life," Dominick recalled. "Her eyes were open, massively enlarged, staring lifelessly up at the ceiling. Her beautiful hair had been shaved off. A large bolt had been screwed into her skull to relieve the pressure on her brain. Her neck was purpled and swollen; vividly visible on it were the marks of the massive hands of the man who had strangled her.

It was nearly impossible to look at her, but also impossible to look away."

The hospital's staff did everything they could for Dunne, and after five days, her parents made the decision to remove her from the life-support systems that were keeping her alive. Dunne died instantly, and her heart and kidneys were donated to the hospital to be used for transplants.

Dunne's tragic death was a shock to the entire Hollywood community, particularly for Dunne's extensive network of family and friends. Hundreds of people attended Dunne's funeral, held on November 6 at the catholic Church of the Good Shepherd in Beverly Hills – the same church where Dunne had been baptized 22 years earlier. Her body was laid to rest near Los Angeles, at the Westwood Memorial Park.

## "An act of passion and despair."

"If (Dunne) had been killed in an automobile accident, horrible as that would have been, at least it would have been over and mourning could have begun," Dominick said. "A murder is an ongoing event until the day of the sentencing, and mourning has to be postponed."

Sweeney was charged with Dunne's murder, and the case finally went to trial at the court in Santa Monica in early August, 1983. A *People* magazine article from October 1983 described Sweeney as a "young man in a black suit" seated at a long table, his face "white as an egg" and his large, pale hands "folded meekly" over a Bible.

"It is the fashion among the criminal fraternity to find God, and Sweeney, the killer, was no exception," Dominick remembered. "The Bible was a prop; Sweeney never read it, he just rested his folded hands on it. He also wept regularly. One day, the court had to be recessed because he claimed the other prisoners had been harassing before he entered, and he needed time to cry in private.

"I could not believe that the jurors would buy such a performance."

But Sweeney painted a very different picture in the courtroom than the true colors he'd shown to Dunne's family and friends. According to Sweeney's testimony, Dunne "provoked" the violent struggle that resulted in her death, because she had previously agreed to reconcile and had then refused to take Sweeney back. Sweeney said he "just exploded and lunged toward her" after she told him she'd been lying when she said she would live with him again.

He added that he "had no memory" of the event, only that he found himself next to Dunne's unconscious body, with his hands pressed around her neck. According to Sweeney, he tried to resuscitate her, and when that didn't work, he ran into the house and swallowed two bottles of pills – attempting suicide due to his panic and regret at what he had done.

Sweeney's lawyer Michael Adelson added that Dunne was a "snob," who was constantly telling Sweeney how he was beneath her. Sweeney's account of their relationship presented Dunne as two-faced and heartless, and he said she even told him that she had been leading him on.

Dominick even recalled receiving a phone call from the prosecutor for the case, district attorney Steven Barshop, in July, shortly before the trial was set to begin. Barshop explained that Adelson had requested that Lenny not be allowed in the courtroom – Adelson felt the presence of the victim's mother, confined to a wheelchair, would create "undue sympathy for her that would be prejudicial to Sweeney."

The "accident" was a "tragedy," Adelson argued, "not a real crime – an action of passion and despair."

However, no evidence could be found to back up Sweeney's story, and investigators were reluctant to believe him. There was nothing to support Sweeney's claim that he'd attempted to commit suicide, and even during his initial interrogation, Sweeney seemed to show little remorse for his part in Dunne's death.

In fact, the police officers who arrested him testified that Sweeney had seemed "quite calm and collected," and more concerned about what would happen to him than what had happened to Dunne – only about an hour and a half after he'd been arrested.

"I fucked up, I can't believe I did something that will put me behind bars forever," Sweeney reportedly told police when he was brought down to the station. "Man, I blew it. I killed her. I didn't think I choked her that hard. I just kept on choking her. I just lost my temper and blew it again."

When one of the officers made a comment about how well Dunne had been doing with her acting career, Sweeney retorted, "well, I was doing quite well in *my* career. I'm quite proud of what I've done."

Upon further investigation, it was revealed that Sweeney had obviously strangled Dunne for about five minutes – at least four minutes, according to the medical examiner. According to police, this makes Sweeney's story fairly improbable. Not only would Sweeney have had enough time to realize what he was doing while he was choking his ex-girlfriend, he would have had the opportunity to regain control and let Dunne live.

During the trial, Dominick remembers Barshop holding up a hand to the jury, silencing the room for a four-minute period – "how long it took for Dominique Dunne to die," Barshop said, in his opening statement.

"It was horrifying," Dominick said. "I had never allowed myself to think how long she had struggled in his hands, thrashing for life. A gunshot or a knife stab is over in an instant; strangulation is an eternity."

Barshop also brought forward testimony from one of Sweeney's previous girlfriends – a secretary named Lillian Pierce, who'd also lived with Sweeney. During their relationship, which lasted from 1977 to 1980, he'd abused her on at least ten different occasions – resulting in two separate hospital visits, one for a perforated eardrum and collapsed lung, and a second time with a broken nose.

"Later, we heard that (Pierce) had sat in a car outside the church at (Dunne's) funeral and cried," Dominick said, "feeling too guilty to go inside."

The testimony proved that unlike what Sweeney's lawyer had argued, this was not a unique crime of passion, but rather a pattern of abusive behaviour toward women. Still, Sweeney's lawyer was able to convince the judge that the testimony was prejudicial, and had it excluded from the trial.

"Her account of her relationship with John Sweeney was so shocking that it should have put to rest forever the defense stand that the strangulation death of Dominique Dunne at the hands of John Sweeney was an isolated incident," wrote Dominick. "He was, it became perfectly apparent, a classic abuser of women – and his weapon was his hands."

As he questioned Pierce, without the jury present, Adelson inquired about a specific discussion the witness had had with himself and another lawyer on November 3, 1982 – the day before Dunne was officially removed from life-support and pronounced legally dead.

"Even while (Dunne) lay dying, efforts were being made to free her killer by men who knew very well that this was not his first display of violence," Dominick said. "I felt hatred for Michael Adelson. His object was to win; nothing else mattered."

Testimonies from Dunne's friends and co-workers were also ruled out after Sweeney's lawyer argued that they were nothing but hearsay. These statements explained that Dunne was not remotely interested in a reconciliation with Sweeney – in fact, she'd spent the final five weeks of her life in "permanent fear" of her abusive ex-boyfriend.

Even without this important evidence, the prosecution still sought a second-degree murder conviction, with a minimum sentence of fifteen years.

The jury did get to hear a letter found by Dunne's friends, addressed to Sweeney but obviously never sent to him. The letter detailed Dunne's frustrations at the control Sweeney attempted to hold over her, and her desire to end the relationship.

"You do not love me. You are obsessed with me. The person you think you love is not me at all. It is someone you have made up in your head," Dunne said in her letter. "I'm the person who makes you angry, who you fight with sometimes. I think we only fight when images of me fade away and you are faced with the real me.

"The whole thing has made me realize how scared I am of you, and I don't mean just physically. I'm afraid of the next time you are going to have another mood swing. When we are good, we are great. But when we are bad, we are horrendous. The bad outweighs the good."

**An unsatisfying result**

The trial wrapped up at the end of September, and the jury found Sweeney guilty of voluntary manslaughter – to the shock of Dunne's family and friends. "The law protected him," the jury said, but several members later admitted that had they known about Sweeney's history of violence and abuse, they would have found him guilty of the second-degree murder charge.

"I guess there is never any real satisfaction that the legal system can give, but this – the outcome – was such a blow, such a slap in the face to our family and to (Dunne's) memory," said Dunne's older brother Griffin. "They literally got away with murder... the bitterness of that will never leave."

Even Superior Court Judge Burton S. Katz, who presided over the trial, felt the system failed to provide justice for Dunne's tragic murder. Barshop stated that this failure has allowed a "time bomb" to return to the streets, where he could potentially abuse again, and blames Katz for the many rulings he made that prohibited the jury from hearing important, relevant evidence.

However, Katz argued that he had no choice but to rule the way he had – but admitted that some of the more controversial rulings during the trial "pained" him. Shortly after Sweeney's trial, Katz moved to the Juvenile Court in Sylmar.

"Nothing is more difficult than rendering a decision based upon a law with which you disagree," Katz said. "Unfortunately, following the letter of the law sometimes doesn't permit one to pursue the ultimate goal of justice."

Sweeney ended up with a sentence of only six and a half years in prison, the maximum sentence imposed for convictions of voluntary manslaughter. Instead of the fifteen years the prosecution had hoped for, Sweeney was released from a medium-security state prison after spending three years, seven months, and twenty-seven days in custody.

"Three and a half years for a life is certainly not justice," Katz said. "If I could have given him 25 (years), I would have given him 25. If I could have given him life, I would have given him life... I agree with everyone that based on his past record of violence... he is dangerous to any woman."

Soon after his release from prison, Sweeney found another high-paying job as a head chef at a chic restaurant in Santa Monica called "The Chronicle." The new position didn't last long, though -

Sweeney was fired after Dunne's family and friends descended on the restaurant with handbills that were distributed to guests and passers-by.

"The hands that prepared your food strangled Dominique Dunne on October 30, 1982," the handbills read.

Sweeney left Los Angeles for Seattle in 1989, and changed his name to John Maura. According to some sources, he is currently employed there as an executive chef for a chain restaurant.

"This guy gets to be reinstated as the head chef in a restaurant as if nothing ever happened," said Dunne's older brother, actor Griffin Dunne. "If she had lived, she'd be an actress everyone in the world would know... he's a murderer; he's murdered and I think he will do it again."

Another friend of the family echoed these thoughts, adding that "the verdict almost says it's okay to kill the one you love."

# THE MURDER OF FAITH HEDGEPETH

# JESSI DAVIS

**Happy-go-lucky**

In 1982, Connie Hedgepeth had her hands full with two teenage daughters and a husband who was addicted to drugs. Her marriage was struggling when she took a pregnancy test, hoping the result would be negative. It wasn't. Her youngest daughter was born eight months later, and Connie named her Faith.

"I felt like it was my faith in God that helped me through that situation," she said. "My faith helped me to continue to work and to do what I needed to do for my children."

Still, Connie divorced her husband when Faith was still young. Struggling to stay afloat, Connie turned to her oldest daughter, Rolanda, for support. Despite an almost 18-year age difference, Rolanda and Faith developed a strong bond – "part mother-daughter, part sister," Rolanda explained.

"We were always close. I was kind of like a second mom, but there was that sister bond, too," she said.

Rolanda's daughter Alexis was born on Faith's first birthday, and the two girls grew up together in rural North Carolina. Her upbringing was difficult, but Faith's positive attitude and eagerness to contribute propelled her through her schooling. She was an honor student, a cheerleader, and a regular volunteer for many other clubs and organizations.

"She always had this energy about her," Rolanda recalled. "She was really happy-go-lucky."

Faith's father had dropped out of college to raise his family, and Faith intended to pick up where her dad had left off. She earned a Gates Millennium Scholarship to the University of North Carolina at Chapel Hill – the very school her father had been attending. Poised to be the very first college graduate in her family, Faith had plans to become a pediatrician or a teacher once she completed her education.

Instead, the Native American biology major never made it to her 20th birthday. Police records reveal that Faith was last seen alive at approximately 3 a.m. on September 7, 2012, when she and her roommate Karena Rosario came home after an evening partying at a local nightclub.

### The Thrill of a lifetime

The night before she was murdered, Faith had been studying with Karena at the Davis Library, on the university campus. At around 8 or 8:30 p.m., Faith took a break from her studies to send a text to her father – "Hey Daddy, I love you," the message read. She also texted her niece, reminding her to register to vote in the upcoming election.

At around midnight, the girls left the library and stopped back at their apartment before heading out at approximately 1 a.m. to arrive at a nightclub called The Thrill.

Just after 2:30 a.m., the girls left the bar. Karena was feeling sick after having had too much to drink, and wanted to go home. Faith helped Karena get into bed, and then fell asleep herself. However, a text message from Faith's phone was received at 3:40 a.m. by Brandon Edwards, Karena's ex-boyfriend.

"Hey b. can you come over here please," the message read. "Karena needs you more aha. You know. Please let her know you care."

A few minutes later, another text comes through that simply says, "than." It is suspected that the message was intended to fix a typo in the original message, correcting it to say "Karena needs you more *than* you know." Brandon didn't reply until the next day, when Faith's phone received a text at 4:16 p.m. that read, "Who is this?"

At around 4:30 a.m., Karena left the apartment to go over to a friend's house – and claims that she did see Faith asleep at that time. When she returned at around 11 a.m., however, she found her roommate's body in her room, in her bed, "covered by a blanket on top of her slightly askew mattress with large amounts of blood."

At 11:01 a.m., a 911 call came from the house.

Faith was unconscious and cold, Karena told the dispatcher who took the call, and there was "blood everywhere." She said she thought there may have been an altercation, explaining to the dispatcher that "there were items in the room that were not hers and that it looked like someone else had been there."

Police responded immediately, securing the scene at the girls' apartment complex and collecting evidence. They found Faith's body "positioned on the floor, leaning against the bed, with her shirt pulled up and no clothes from the waist down."

Medical examiners concluded that the cause of death was blunt force trauma, based on the severe beating Faith had endured. When the autopsy report was unsealed nearly two years after the killing, it was revealed that she also had bruises and cuts all over her arms and legs, as well as blood underneath her fingernails.

"It's very, very hard, learning of how Faith died," said Rolanda. "She was beaten, she was bludgeoned to death. A lot of people don't understand what that means, but it was really bad."

A rape kit had also been performed, indicating the presence of semen – with DNA that matched other DNA that police had recovered at the scene. Law enforcement officials have not confirmed whether the sexual activity was consensual or forced.

**Searching for suspects**

In the years since Faith's death, multiple search warrants have been executed – as well as numerous court orders for things like cell phones, computers, and even social media accounts. DNA testing has also been carried out on many of men that interacted with Karena and Faith while they were at the nightclub, but so far, investigators have found no matching results.

While at The Thrill, Faith was reportedly dancing with a man named David Bell. He told police he didn't know Faith very well, and was not named by police as a suspect during the investigation.

"(Redacted) was identified as walking out of Club Thrill with Faith Hedgepeth shortly before the homicide occurred," read a police report unsealed in 2014. "He was the last male to be seen with her before her death."

The report added that Bell admitted to talking with Faith the night she was killed, and to meeting her the weekend before. He refused to provide investigators with a sample of his DNA, claiming that he had likely touched her at some point during the night of the homicide. His statements to law enforcement officers were also determined to be "inconsistent" with statements provided by others.

Another man, Jacob Beatley, was interviewed by police and also not named as a suspect. Karena visited him during the early morning hours of September 7, after leaving the apartment she shared with Faith. DNA was also sought from a man named Reginald Leonard Jackson II, who was not named as a suspect despite having been texting regularly with Faith in the days prior to her murder.

However, none of this information was offered to Faith's family until the documents were unsealed in 2014.

"All they have said to us and to the public, to the media, to everybody, (is) that this wasn't random – how do they know that?" said Chad Hedgepeth, Faith's brother. "Do they have a suspect? Do they have any suspects? ... Tell us something, because being in the dark on any and everything these past four weeks has been brutal."

While the recording from the 911 call seems to indicate that Karena was alone when she discovered Faith's body in their apartment, the police report stated that she returned to their home with a friend. In the recording, however, Karena consistently claims "I just walked into my apartment," instead of saying "we." There is also no sound recorded that could be attributed to another person in the room.

An analysis of the call could suggest that the repetition of the statement "I just walked into my apartment" is an attempt to establish an alibi – especially since the recording reveals that Karena says this several times before even providing the dispatcher with necessary information like the victim's state or the location of the emergency.

At no point in the call does Karena specifically ask for help for the victim. She also apologizes to the dispatcher, using language that analysts typically see in calls where guilty knowledge is indicated.

Initially, law enforcement turned their attention to Eriq Takoy Jones – an ex-boyfriend of Karena's who lived in the same apartment complex and was reportedly an aspiring rapper. Just a few months before the murder, Karena had filed a restraining order against Eriq, on the basis of domestic assault. Police had previously investigated claims that Eriq had kicked two of the doors in the girls' apartment completely off their frames, and eyewitness accounts reported that Karena had been seen with visible injuries to her body – inflicted, she said, by her ex-boyfriend.

"Faith took Karena to take out a restraining order," said Faith's father, Roland Hedgepeth. "I think that very possibly, Takoy may have had some ill feelings toward Faith for doing that."

Rolanda said Faith had moved in with Karena after the restraining order had been filed, to help her friend as she recovered from the abusive relationship.

"I wasn't worried about Faith at the time," Rolanda said. "I wanted them to be safe. I just wanted both of them to be safe."

Just before Faith was murdered, Eriq posted a chilling message on his Facebook page, and texted a similar message to an acquaintance.

"Deal Lord," the post read. "Forgive me for all of my sins and the sins I may commit today. Protect me from the girls who don't deserve me and the ones who wish me dead today."

An unnamed person who claimed to be a former roommate of Faith's called the Chapel Hill Police Department the day after Faith's body was discovered with additional concerning information about Eriq. According to the caller, Faith had told her that Karena's boyfriend hated her (Faith) and told her that if Karena wouldn't get back together with him, he would kill Faith.

However, Eriq was very cooperative with law enforcement during the investigation into Faith's murder. Both his apartment and car were combed for trace evidence, and his DNA was tested and cleared.

"From what I knew of her (Faith), she was the sweetest person in the world. If you needed her and she could do it, she was there," Eriq told news reporters after Faith's murder. "I'll be honest with you – whoever did this deserves to burn."

Investigators also learned that the ex-boyfriend of Karena's that Faith had texted in the hours before she was killed had also been present that night at The Thrill. Police records indicated that Brandon Edwards had even spent the night at the girls' apartment the night before the murder – making his response to Faith's texts the day she was killed quite unusual.

According to a friend named Marisol Rangel, Karena and Brandon were "just friends" at the time of Faith's murder. Marisol is the friend who was reportedly with Karena when she discovered Faith's body, but the 911 operator was confident that Karena was alone when the call was placed.

In January 2013, police released a profile of the killer. According to the profile, developed by Chapel Hill Police and the FBI's Behavioral Analysis Unit, the person responsible for Faith's murder might have been familiar with her – and possibly even lived near her in the past.

The individual may have also "made comments" about Faith in the past, with their behavior shifting after the murder occurred. Obviously, the profile indicated this person would have been "unaccounted for" during the early morning hours of September 7, 2012. Police also stated the DNA evidence collected at the scene of the homicide points toward a "male suspect."

At the time, Faith's father Roland said the development of the profile marked a "new beginning" in the investigation, and believed it would help police solve the case.

"For us, we're kind of stuck back on September 7," he said. "Every day, we get up and relive that day. But I'm confident things will open up soon."

**Strange evidence**

Nearly two years after the murder, police released a shocking and mysterious piece of evidence. A spiteful, handwritten note was found scrawled on a fast food bag left near the crime scene, with the words "I'M NOT STUPID BITCH JEALOUS."

Police believe the note was written by the killer, but have not said whether the handwriting has ever been officially analyzed. According to private investigator and forensic handwriting examiner Peggy Walla, some clues can be determined from the note.

"What struck me was how clean the document is – the crime scene was pretty bloody, and there's nothing on this document," she said. "Looking at it, I would get the impression it was either written outside of the crime scene, or it was written before, like a premeditation."

She also feels the words were written by a non-dominant hand, indicating that whoever wrote the note was attempting to "disguise" their penmanship. The block letters could be taken as the writer's attempt to distance themselves from authority, she said.

"The word and sentence phrase 'I'm not stupid' is a hot push-button factor," Walla added. "That's probably the most important thing said. This was a jealous person who was called 'stupid.' The person that said it who is now deceased has no way of repeating this person is stupid, which is another way to shut them up."

Users of online forums have also speculated that the use of the word 'jealous' could indicate that the writer of the note was a woman, as the word is thought to be more frequently used by females. The formation of the letter 'P' in particular has also struck some as seeming feminine in nature.

Other speculation surrounds the intent of the note. The words 'jealous' and 'bitch' suggest that the note was not meant for the police of for the public – rather, these deeply personal words were likely intended toward Faith, or possibly even Karena, who would eventually find the body. But more curious yet is the situation that must have occurred that led to the writing of the note. What happened before Faith was murdered?

### Cries for help

A clue may be found in a voicemail left for a friend the night of her death. The call appears to have been a pocket-dial – a very timely pocket-dial that potentially recorded the final minutes of Faith's life. The timestamp on the nearly unintelligible message indicates that the call was made while Faith was still at The Thrill, but some have argued that a glitch in technology could have resulted in an incorrect time.

According to President and CEO of Creative Forensic Services Arlo West, who is certified by the New York Institute of Forensic Audio in enhancement, authentication, and analysis of both audio and video, the names 'Rosie' and 'Eriq' appear throughout the recording – potentially referring to Karena Rosario and her ex-boyfriend Eriq Takoy Jones.

"I've worked on hundreds, if not thousands, of cases where people have pocket-dialed somebody," West said. "If you can peel back those layers of noise, you start to get a better picture of the dialogue that is contained – stuff that starts to make a little more sense."

In his analysis for Crime Watch Daily, West identified two distinct female voices – one which he claimed is Faith Hedgepeth, and the other he describes as a "very angry female." He also picked out at least two male voices.

"I hear what I believe is Miss Hedgepeth's cries for help," West said. "You can hear her emotive voice, the tone of her voice, is clearly in pain ... You can clearly hear what I believe is Faith pleading. She's being hurt, being attacked."

West said he feels "very confident" about hearing the names 'Rosie' and 'Eriq,' and included both names in his transcript of the three-minute recording.

He also claims iPhones were "inherently problematic with timestamping" during the time Faith was killed – which he said accounts for the timestamp on the voicemail showing 1:23 a.m., while police believe Faith was killed sometime after 4:30 a.m. Still, Chapel Hill police did contact West for an official analysis of the recording.

"If it is Faith being murdered, and captured in this recording – which I think it is, this is pivotal," West said. "It should be able to solve this case."

Police seem to believe that the voicemail was recorded from the club, not from the apartment – and in the middle of the call, there appears to be music playing or someone rapping. There is also no evidence to support that the name 'Rosie' could have referred to Karena, and Eriq Takoy Jones was apparently called 'Takoy' by his friends.

Still, the voicemail is difficult to discount – especially since, on the night Faith was murdered, it appears to have recorded an emotionally-charged, angry discussion. To many listeners, including members of Faith's family, the voices sound agitated – belligerent, fast-speaking – and seem to be punctuated by audible yelps of what could be pain.

"From day one, I heard my daughter screaming in the background," said Faith's father, Roland. "I knew something was going on."

**"A really good case."**

The note, the voicemail audio, and other documents – including the 15-page autopsy – were unsealed in September 2014. According to Chris Blue, Chapel Hill Police Chief, the effort was an attempt to generate new leads in the investigation.

"We have excellent evidence – we have a really good case," he said. "We just need to connect this really good case with the killer."

However, in those two years, police had been unable to connect any potential suspect with the crime. The official documents were sealed during that time despite repeated requests from lawyers and news organizations to open them to the public, as investigators felt releasing the information would compromise their efforts.

"It's not that it might hinder this investigation, it will hinder this investigation," said Durham County Assistant District Attorney Charlene Franks.

She added that details contained within the documents, including the 911 call where the crime scene and body are vividly described, could help police identify the killer – as that information would have been known by very few people.

In a "cold case," Franks said, police will often turn to the public for assistance. However, since the investigation into Faith's murder is ongoing, solving the case means keeping the public – including Faith's family – in the dark about some vital details.

"The most important thing to them and the state and the Chapel Hill Police Department is to find the killer of their baby girl, Faith Hedgepeth," she said. "The only way to do that is to keep those items sealed because the information contained in there, other than (investigators), only the killer knows."

According to Steve Hale, private investigator and retired homicide detective who was never involved with the case, it's typical for law enforcement to keep the details of a case under wraps – interviews and tips that haven't been influenced by media reports can make or break a case.

"If there is a suspect, he may not know he's a suspect, and they're waiting for him to get careless and maybe make a comment to an accessory after the fact," he said, adding that detectives likely suspected someone who knew Faith and might have had a distinct motive.

Each document pertaining to the case was reviewed by Judge Howard Manning before being unsealed in 2014. Still, three investigators with the Chapel Hill Police Department and State Bureau of Investigation continued working exclusively on the unsolved case – and offered a reward of $40,000 for any information leading to the arrest and conviction of Faith's killer.

"We really want to bring some peace to Faith's family," said Blue. "This has been two unimaginable years for them."

**"Your imagination starts to run wild."**

Connie was contacted three hours after Faith's body was found, by a crisis counselor who told her little more than that her 19-year-old daughter Faith had been found dead in her apartment – the victim of what appeared to be a violent homicide.

"I said, 'you must have the wrong girl,'" Connie remembers. "She told me it was her, and I said, 'I don't think so.'"

It fell on Connie to contact the rest of the family, spreading the devastating news to her son, her ex-husband, and her eldest daughter, Rolanda. At that point, Connie said, she didn't have much to tell them other than that Faith was dead.

"They couldn't tell us very much because they didn't want to jeopardize the investigation," she explained. "Not knowing anything at all... your imagination starts to run wild."

Even after detectives brought the family to Chapel Hill, about 80 miles away from their home in Hollister, Connie still had no answers to her many questions. She wasn't even permitted to visit the crime scene, or see her youngest daughter.

"I just wanted to hold her hand, to let her know I was there," Connie recalled. "I still cry for my baby, and I wonder if she called out for help. Did she cry for me? These are the things you think."

Finally, the family was told the cause of death – but without any kind of motive or indication of what could have happened to lead up to Faith's murder, the new information was difficult for the family to process.

"It is getting harder, not knowing what happened, trying to accept what happened," said Rolanda. "She was beautiful. She didn't deserve it. She had a lot going for her."

While no arrests have been made, and no suspects even identified, Chapel Hill Police Lt. Josh Mecimore said police are still confident that the killer will be found and brought to justice.

"Someone knows something, and we're continually appealing to the public to come forward," he said. "This is not a cold case. We are still following up on things, still pounding the pavement, still waiting for that one piece of evidence that will help us solve this case."

Connie, Rolanda, and the rest of the Hedgepeth family are clinging to the same hope.

"At some point, God will let us know what happened," Rolanda said. "Even when I'm down, I still believe that we will find that person."

However, neighbours remain concerned as a result of the limited information available – and the fact that police have yet to make an arrest. While law enforcement officers continued to reassure nearby residents that the incident was an isolated event, neighbours wanted more answers.

"It's not a reassuring thought to wonder if you can send your kids to safety to the bus stop or if something could happen," said Anna Salomon, who lived with her husband and children in the subdivision next to the apartment complex where Faith was murdered. In the weeks following the killing, the neighbours banded together to walk children to the bus stop in collective groups.

**Keeping Faith alive**

One year after Faith was killed, students at the University of North Carolina gathered on campus at the Bell Tower Amphitheatre for a silent walk in celebration of the student's life. She was also made an honorary member of the Alpha Pi Omega Sorority, the country's oldest Native American Greek letter organization.

"She was the happiest person I knew, always laughing, always smiling," said Faith's friend Leslie Locklear.

Another friend, Victoria Chavis, remembered Faith's "bubbly personality."

"She had a smile that was just infectious," she said, "and she was a wonderful person to be around."

"The entire Carolina community grieves for the loss of this promising, vibrant student," added UNC Chancellor Carol Folt.

The family has honored Faith's memory by establishing the "Faith's Smile Scholarship" in her name – an award which will go to Native American women entering their freshman year of college. The scholarship project gives the family something positive to focus on while they continue searching for answers.

"It's really hard – hard because of not knowing what happened and not knowing why it happened, who did it," Rolanda added. "One little piece of information could break the case, could give us some type of peace. How could somebody withhold that, after everything we have lost?"

Still, for Connie, nothing can extinguish the shining light that defined her youngest daughter, Faith – no matter how many years go by with the case remaining unsolved.

"We don't want anyone to forget her smile. She was a beautiful girl, she was my baby," Connie said. "Her spirit is right here today."

9 798224 091256